Managing Your Personal Brand

Evelyn Verdugo

Managing Your Personal Brand

First Edition: 2022

ISBN: 9781524318277
ISBN eBook: 9781524328252

© of the text:
 Evelyn Verdugo

© Layout, design and production of this edition: 2022 EBL

All rights reserved. No part of this publication may be reproduced, distributed, or transmitted in any form or by any means, including photocopying, recording, or other electronic or mechanical methods, without the prior written permission of the Publisher.

I'm grateful for the life circumstances that have allowed me to share this book with you, my readers. I hope it will raise your awareness of all you are and all you have to offer the world. Thank you to all those who have given me their genuine trust to accompany them in their challenges and projects.

I dedicate this book to my beautiful family in appreciation of their unconditional support on each step of my journey. Thank you for making me feel loved.

Finally, I thank my parents and siblings for showing me the importance of family.

"The time to be happy is now"

Evelyn Verdugo P.

Table of Contents

Foreword 13
Be the Protagonist of Your Own Story 19
    Aware of the Footprint We Leave Behind 22
Personal Brand, Personal Image and Personal Branding 24
Personal Branding Model 28
    Behavioral Dimension 30
    Dimension of Emotions and Emotional Intelligence 31
    Personality Dimension 33
    Coaching Tools 36
    Mentoring Tools 37
Chapter 1. Identification 39
    Success Starts with You 39
    Beliefs 40
    Values 44
    Wheel of Life 49
    Mobilizing Questions 51
Chapter 2. Define Your Personal Brand 53
    What Image Do You Want to Build and Project? 53
    Purpose 54
    Goals 57
    Action Plan 59
    Personal Image 62
    Mobilizing Questions 68
Chapter 3. Skills and Resources 71
    Supporting Your Personal Brand 71
    Skills 72

FOAR Tool 74
Resources 76
Mobilizing Questions 77

Chapter 4. Differentiation 79
What Makes You More Visible? 79
1. Authenticity 81
2. Passion 82
3. Life History 84
4. How You Communicate 85
5. Never Stop Learning 86
6. Self-care 86
From Idea to Action 87
Value Proposition 89
Mobilizing Questions 93

Chapter 5. Competitiveness 95
"Don't Worry, Get Busy." 95
Responsibility 97
Commitment 98
Learning 99
Good Habits 100
How Can We Identify Our Competencies? 102
Mobilizing Questions 104

Chapter 6. The Key to Success 106
Primary Elements in Communication 110
Active Listening 116
Secondary Elements in Communication 123
Mobilizing Questions 125

Chapter 7. Living Your Personal Brand 127
Personal and Professional Image 128
Verbal and Nonverbal Communication in Action ... 129
Presentations 133

    Fear of Public Speaking 133
    Elaboration of the Elevator Pitch 133
    Mobilizing Questions 135
Principles of Personal Branding 137
Bibliography 138

Foreword

This book came about thanks to the quarantine and the endless questions the author asked herself during that period. It also exists thanks to the moments of uncertainty caused by the unusual circumstances that have become the daily experience of the last decade.

Some time ago, I had the opportunity to see the video my father made of my birth, and one of the things that caught my attention was my unrestrained crying. It was like a kind of call of the wild or, if I think of it more analytically, perhaps it was an expression of "please just leave me here in my comfort zone."

With very little hair and little to offer, we must assume that we come into this world for more than one reason, but the best thing is to realize that our psyche is willing to do anything, even self-destruct. Many people become paralyzed when facing a situation of conflict, primarily due to social and cultural causes. In contrast, others manage to see adversity as an opportunity to make themselves stand out from others and develop new skills, not worrying about what people will think or the demands of a strict and unfair society, which is capable of stripping away our true essence.

The opportunity to submerge myself in this book has granted me the possibility of taking meaningful action. Presumably my past is often the root of my fears and insecurities, but, without a doubt, we are always influenced by our surroundings as social beings. As such, we will face uncertainty and situations that will provide positive learning opportunities, despite the negative sensations they may cause. Being present for the good and the bad is essential for dealing with your problems, fears, insecurities, and yearnings. I have come to recognize that our experiences - where we come from and where we want to go - are just the first part of what enables us to empower ourselves from the inside out by forcing us to ground ourselves, be realistic, and consider the tools we have to work with to achieve the goals we set for ourselves, either in the short or the long term.

The learning we gain from these situations makes us begin to trust in our abilities. Furthermore, the experience allows us to recognize the importance of cultivating the instruments required for our evolution as human beings, assuming we are responsible for what we project and that we are versatile people capable of achieving self-knowledge, which is essential to feeling satisfied in all our facets.

I simply want to thank the author of this book for trusting me and helping me reaffirm that life's coincidences exist. This work came into my hands at a time of great uncertainty on a professional level, and one of the things that I will never forget is that we constantly have to decipher our experiences, give ourselves time to analyze them, and become stronger because of them. I remember the author told me that she had a poster in the bedroom she shared with her older sister when she was a child that said, "The time to be happy is now." It was at the foot of her bed. She saw it every time she woke up, and she repeated that phrase to herself over and over again. She became convinced of the veracity of this phrase, and it became a kind of empowering affirmation. The phrase stayed with her because the time to be happy is now. If not now, when?

This *Personal Branding* Model will give you a time of personal connection to find the true meaning of your life, contemplate what you want, and need, to act coherently in all your roles and contexts without question. No one but you has the responsibility to change your path.

The author of this book is passionate about the world of self-knowledge and all that it entails. She invites us to be part of this transformation that will open the doors to what's important to you, following your values, beliefs, and life purpose.

Words tend to be more fluid when the mind is immersed in questioning.

Paulina Mérida Gaete

Journalist

Be the Protagonist of Your Own Story

As I have progressed in my work, I have felt more powerful the vision of delivering a comprehensive view that incorporates the knowledge and experiences acquired during my personal and professional life. My professional life has developed in the areas of sales, administration, finance, *coaching* and consulting. Their union has allowed me to design a *personal branding* model with the objective of facilitating elements that contribute to the development of the personal brand and its management based on our self-knowledge. This model allows us to broaden the vision we have of ourselves, strongly impacting our self-conceptualization and self-esteem and empowering us, putting our skills at the service of what we need in the different contexts in which we find ourselves. This way we will maintain a great self-motivational and adaptive power in front of the challenges we face, making the personal brand shine in an authentic way.

Throughout history, great thinkers have focused on the relevance of the concept of knowing oneself. From the testimony of the famous Greek traveler Pausanias, we learn that in the temple of Apollo, where the famous oracle of Delphi is located, the phrase "know thyself" is inscribed. It is written in gold, right at the entrance of the temple where it is impossible to miss. This was the principle that founded the thinking of philosophers such as Plato, Socrates, Pythagoras and Aristotle.

"Self-knowledge is the first step to all wisdom" - Aristotle.

Through a clear structure, this *personal branding* model provides us with elements to advance self-knowledge. It requires time, dedication, commitment and responsibility, understanding that it is a continuous daily process. This is the basis for the construction and improvement of a personal image that makes us more autonomous and independent. This will be reflected in the definition of clear goals and greater effectiveness and assertiveness in decision making, which affects all areas of life.

"I believe deeply in the abilities of each person; I become part of their self-knowledge and generate awareness to achieve their personal and professional purpose".

I'll tell you part of my story. In 2012, I started my business under the name of Modernas Tentaciones. My knowledge of financial management allowed me to work, in Chile, for an international brand of handbags and accessories.

As the business grew, I saw that my clients were in search of a space where they could receive advice, both personal and image. Apparently, they didn't just come for a bag! That's how I started to build a team that could offer a complete service, a space where clients received dedication and attention they were craving.

I incorporated tools to support both the emotions and the efforts of my team. That is how I earned my certification as a *coach* and a diploma in *life coaching*. Part of this has been reflected in the book *Miradas del coach integrativo. Vol. 2*, edited by Isaías Sharon; where, as co-author I focus on the importance of active listening in *coaching* processes.

Holding the role of VP of Communications on the board of AICI (International Association of Image Consultants) in Chile, has enabled and facilitated contact, both personally and professionally, with people from different cultures, which has shown me that we all have a strong desire to strengthen and empower ourselves to build our projects in various fields, based on what we really are. Currently, as president of AICI Chile, I have new challenges and purposes to achieve for the growth of AICI Chile.

In my continuous search to acquire new skills to better support my clients, I became certified in emotional intelligence. This path has been full of new experiences that I will be able to share and make them available to all those who want to take this journey of personal growth.

I have constantly had the urge to communicate my experience and trajectory. This has allowed me to participate in lectures, diploma courses and radio programs where, along with other professionals, I have addressed issues of personal growth, delivering my view as an expert *coach* in *personal branding* and effective communication.

"I have the conviction that when you differentiate yourself from others you awaken interest in yourself, your project or your business."

People fail or succeed in some aspects of life, not always because of their abilities and skills, but because individuals are influenced by the negative or positive evaluation and assessment of others. Not taking the time to work on our self-knowledge makes it possible to validate those judgments without being clearly aware of what we are.

"Don't let the noise of other people's opinions silence your inner voice. Most importantly, have the courage to do what your heart and intuition tell you to do. In a way, you already know what you really want to become." – Daniel Goleman.

We know what we like or dislike in other people; we judge the abilities and weaknesses in others according to our beliefs, without stopping to consider ourselves and that we may not have the skills to achieve our own goals. Thus, we accumulate diplomas pretending that this is the only way to make us competitive, to ensure our success, assuming that we must invest a lot of time and money.

We hear countless times the famous phrase: "if you don't study, you will be nobody in life", this leads us to study a profession that will make us visible in our personal environment and later in the world. Is it really what we need to be valued? Is this above our identity? Is your value in your professional degree?

Thus, the skills associated with knowledge or learned through professional training—known as hard skills—are not entirely sufficient to be competent; we need to pay attention to other differentiating elements, and it is essential to focus on the skills associated with social relations and emotion, our soft skills. These are made up of communication, interpersonal and behavioral skills, among others. Having these skills makes a difference when relating to others that goes beyond our cognitive knowledge.

In order to build our *personal branding*, it is necessary to identify which skills we have and which ones we will have to use in order to advance in each of the proposed goals. Self-knowledge, planning, setting objectives, developing communication strategies, defining goals become a priority, without forgetting the design of the different platforms to be used both physically and virtually to develop our visibility. All this requires a high personal commitment.

Aware of the Footprint We Leave Behind

In this model of *personal branding*, three fundamental dimensions come together: behavior, emotional intelligence and personality. This set determines how we think, how we relate to people and our general behavior. By becoming aware of each individually as well as how they connect, we will have an integral concept of who we are, visualizing in a clearer and more assertive way what differentiates us from others and admitting our real potential.

The center of the *personal branding* model is, as its name suggests, the person, where the basic concept is to gain confidence and security, achieving a clear management of your personal brand with autonomy and adaptability. With all this, we gather the elements to recognize, structure and manage our personal brand, here the correct use of our talents to reach a concrete result that will push us towards our desires. Our *personal branding* must be firm and cohesive to support our essence. However, at the same time, it must be flexible to be able to adapt to multiple situations and contexts. I compare it to the spine, which has a firm structure capable of supporting the entire body yet is flexible to enable movement.

As you advance through each of the stages of the model, you will strengthen all of them, linking them in such a way that you will make your actions coherent with your purpose and goal in life, without sacrificing your own values or beliefs, but adapting and using them in different areas.

"The more you learn, the more you have to give."

Personal Brand, Personal Image and Personal Branding

These three concepts have subtle differences that are important to clarify in order to understand each stage of this model.

The personal brand is our identity, our personal seal, being that mark that we leave with people. It is essential to look for that differentiating element that you have and that you can bring to the world, that makes you stand out. Personal image is what you project, it is what others think of you and how they remember you.

So, what is *personal branding*?

It is the process in which you learn to manage your personal brand and image. It is made up of factors such as essence, experience, the way we relate to others, personality, and more.

The concept of *personal branding* first appears in 1997, in an article published in *Fast Company* called "The brand called you", written by Tom Peters, an American specialist in business management. The author shows us the importance of working on self-knowledge, personal strategy, visibility, personal power, leadership, loyalty, considering your own needs, continuous evaluation and our projects. "You are in charge of your brand".

"That cross-trainer you're wearing — one look at the distinctive swoosh on the side tells everyone who's got you branded. That coffee travel mug you're carrying — ah, you're a Starbucks woman! Your T-shirt with the distinctive Champion

"C" on the sleeve, the blue jeans with the prominent Levi's rivets, the watch with the hey-this-certifies-I-made-it icon on the face, your fountain pen with the maker's symbol crafted into the end ..." Excerpt *Fast Company* 1997.

Later, I will explain how our self-concept and self-knowledge influence this elaboration procedure.

We find different methods and approaches to apply to our *personal branding;* for some, it may be developing a prominent presence on social networks, working on your personal image, fostering your public relations, communicating effectively, and even how to sell ourselves. The approach depends on our own needs which, as a priority, must be defined for greater effectiveness.

Currently, we find ourselves, to a large extent, with a strong focus on social networks and digital *marketing,* where social relations are not only given to a work of personal contact networks, but to generate an influence on the other or to accommodate trends.

The advantage that globalization and digital tools bring us is that they allow us to interact with the whole world without having to move from our desks, giving us the opportunity to explore new cultures and different ways of communication. We also see that learning to communicate and create a common language is paramount in delivering the message we want to convey.

I find it appropriate to define the personal brand as a reflection of your personality, where you naturally differ from other people. Focusing on this will help you to spread the right message and achieve your objectives. This personal strategy requires having self-knowledge as the main basis, to then make visible our real contribution and value, enabling us to contribute to our environment, adapting and evolving with it.

In this way, building our *personal branding becomes a* great ally for successful self-management, reach and credibility. It is the individual identity by which others recognize us and is evidenced in how they remember you. It is built during the trajectory of life, through the observation of each of the experiences that provide us with learning, knowledge, skills and more. It is an X-ray of our person. This is what makes us different, gives us that competitive edge and opens more opportunities to reach our proposed goals.

Personal branding works under the ideal that you intend to achieve and continuously improve yourself. It raises awareness of who we are and what we want, not only as professionals, but as people. Based on this, your brand and personal image are enhanced and adapted in any scenario. This model of *personal branding is* a guide through the path of self-knowledge that will provide you with key pieces to effectively and assertively manage both.

In this model, being the protagonist of your own story makes sense and is put into practice. Here, behavior, identity and knowledge are coherently unified, highlighting the qualities that are essential to move towards our goals, captivating and conquering our environment in a natural and credible way.

In work and social environments, applying the above enables you to define the image you project and how you will be seen. In this way, you will carry out strategies for different contexts, keeping your values and purposes consistent in all environments in which you operate. *Personal branding* will help you manage and protect your brand and personal image. You will be remembered or sought after for that element that makes you different as a person without the need to demonstrate your experience, prove your professional qualifications and awards. When you find these unique aspects and learn to use them to your advantage, you gain confidence, projecting it to others, making you more competitive and positioning yourself as trustworthy and genuine. This awareness makes it easier to align who you are with what you do, always in the direction of your purpose.

This model of *personal branding* focuses on the individual, using tools from various disciplines such as NLP (Neuro-Linguistic Programming), *integrative coaching*, emotional intelligence, image consulting, management, *marketing*, positive psychology, etc., from which I acquired guidelines so that each stage fulfills the objective of bringing you closer to your goals.

Working on *personal branding* goes hand in hand with constant self-discovery, which requires developing habits and behaviors day by day. It is a sincere and open internal communication that broadens the vision of who we are.

This model is a contribution to personal and professional growth, with which you can position yourself with confidence and conviction in any field and, thus, it is at hand to apply it to you and your clients.

"Success starts with you."

Personal Branding Model

Before starting with the description of the model, it is important to stop for a second and consider our past achievements and events that have changed us. Ask yourself these questions; "what was I like before and what was the catalyst for my motivation?" "How did this affect my relationships with other people?" "Have I valued these small changes?"

You already have the answers. Sometimes we do not need to make great efforts to remember: the smell of a place, the perfume of a person or circumstances of life lead you to travel your memories and reflect on that experience for a while. It is a journey that today I invite you to make thinking about the answers you can give to these questions. These answers are the first step on the path to answering the big question: "what is really important to achieve my *personal branding*?"

In today's increasingly competitive society, where everything changes and evolves rapidly, we appreciate the need to trust and feel confident in who we are and what we can contribute to the environment. Building that security will depend on how much we know about ourselves and how much we know about the origin of our behaviors.

We are social beings that grow through interaction with the environment and this, in turn, is cemented within us. As we move through situations in which each person has his or her own customs, behaviors and ideas that have an impact on the other, we generate bonds that take on value in our personal development. We incorporate those behaviors that persist over time, responding to certain situations in a similar way, shaping our personality. These factors, including learning, environment and emotions, condition us when we act, influencing the direction our lives take and the achievement of our goals.

We are bombarded by messages telling us that our success depends on us, that if others can achieve why can't we? But have we been taught to achieve it? It's as if we have the recipe title but not the ingredients. This can lead us to focus on our limitations, negative emotions and makes the achievement of goals less likely as fear takes over. As a result, we become frustrated and immobilized. This is where we realize that emotions also play an important role in the management of situations that arise in this long road of life. Thus, it becomes valuable to have a lighthouse that facilitates the way to find our own potential and achieve what we long for.

This model of *personal branding* is designed covering three dimensions: behavior, emotional intelligence and personality. The model unites tools from various disciplines where each provides elements to facilitate the path of self-knowledge and personal growth, focusing on interaction with others rather than an entirely individualistic path. This way it is possible to effectively manage you brand and personal image according to your values and interests with an awareness of your behavior, emotions and personality.

Behavioral Dimension

Why do we do what we do?

Our behavior is understood as the reactions we have according to the environment or space in which we find ourselves. It is a way of responding to environmental stimuli, whether consciously or unconsciously, voluntarily or involuntarily. It is influenced by various mediated or immediate factors, of the genetic, social, cultural, psychological, economic and affective order. It includes not only behavior as a cognitive process—imagination, thought, memory, perception, sensation—but also aspects that are not as simple to observe as the emotional.

Imagine you are going down a river and suddenly it divides into two streams. You want to go left, but the current leads you to the right. What can you do? Do you let yourself go or do you look for a way to direct your course?

How many times has it happened to us that our behaviors were conditioned by our environment? "Tell me who you hang out with, and I'll tell you who you are". Now that sounds like a very apt phrase. So how do we improve our behaviour? The main thing is to start being more conscious, identifying and understanding the reason(s) we behave in a certain way, what conditions our decision- making processes. Once we understand this, we can understand how to modify our behavior. If this isn't possible then it's important to be more aware of our personal triggers. Thanks to this method, before reaching the division of the two streams, we will already know how to ensure we follow the desired stream.

We must keep in mind the neuroplasticity of our brain, which means that it adapts to our environment and evolves according to multiple factors. Even if an individual is born with the brain of a great musician, it will not develop if not provided with the right environment.

By this I mean that our environment plays a very important role in achieving our goals.

Dimension of Emotions and Emotional Intelligence

What emotion did this situation provoke?

When we throw a stone into a lake it generates waves that are produced in a chain and dissipate in the distance. The impact will depend on the size and force with which the stone hits the water. Emotions, like the stone, influence your environment and the people around you according to their intensity. The outcome can, of course, be positive or negative.

Emotions originate as a response to an external stimulus or an internal event - thought, image, conduct, etc. - which, according to our mental map, we give a value to. The result is a neuropsychological, behavioral or cognitive reaction. Emotions can be contagious. Therefore, it is important to be responsible with them, understanding that they do not only affect us.

We must consider that although the emotions that are considered basic are sadness, joy, anger, surprise, disgust and fear, there are many others that we do not know how to verbalize when they occur. The first step is to examine what provoked that emotion and expand our register of what we feel, many times we do not only experience one emotion, but several together or one after the other, which can cause confusion. Sometimes the same stimulus can cause us to get angry and sad at the same time. Being surprised may provoke joy or fear, depending on the origin of the impulse or the context. Recognizing these patterns makes it easier for us to direct our emotional awareness to open the way to emotional intelligence.

Emotional intelligence is related to the psychological abilities and skills that involve feeling, understanding, controlling and modifying our own and other people's emotions. We are emotionally intelligent when we have the disposition to manage emotions adapting them to communicate and express them in an assertive way.

Emotional intelligence plays a central role in the success or failure of human relationships, from sentimental and family relationships to work relationships. Emotional intelligence also impacts how organizations function. Empathy, emotional self-control and motivation play an important role in how teams work together.

Some people stand out more for the ability to self-manage their emotions than for their cognitive skills. Daniel Goleman's book *Emotional Intelligence offers* a synthesis of the great advantage of a person who is emotionally competent, clearly demonstrating that intelligence goes beyond cognitive abilities.

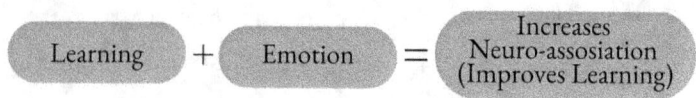

In addition, research conducted in the field of psychology and neuroscience has shown that emotions play a vital role in optimizing learning, since when we associate a stimulus with an emotion, it automatically motivates the integration of that learning.

Personality Dimension

Personality is a construct of repetitive patterns of thoughts, feelings and behaviors that originate from biological, cultural factors, experiences and values. It is the psychological, physical and emotional way of being. It is deeply related to our gregarious life, that is, what we build up in social life and within our environment. The inner organization of these characteristics determines what differentiates us from others, what makes us unique.

Knowing our personality helps us to understand how we react to certain situations, making it easier to manage our behavior effectively.

There are certain positive and negative characteristics of our personality that are inherited. These must also be understood in order to work out how to establish and meet our goals in a realistic manner. An individual who is easily distracted, for example, will struggle to achieve goals that require concentration. Pursuing the unachievable will bring disappointment and even generate a lack of motivation to perform other activities that should be achievable. This does not mean that we are not capable of modifying our behavior. On the contrary, we can acquire and/or modify our personality traits according to the challenges, but this requires personal internal work.

Personality is dynamic; we can modify ourselves and focus on specific traits that benefit us in specific environments.

$$\text{Temperament (genetic)} + \text{Character (cultural)} = \text{Personality}$$

Understanding these three dimensions: behavior, emotion and personality, we can observe in the following image how they are related. Emotion impacts our brain, both the reptilian and limbic, regarding the way we perceive reality. Information is then processed in the neocortex, which affects and mobilizes behavior. The latter defines our personality, which determines our emotion.

In this model of *personal branding*, the three dimensions mentioned above interact, each one having pieces that cohere into a strong, flexible and adaptable gear to forge this so-called "backbone", with the person as the main axis. It is important to remember that we are all unique and unrepeatable, conscious and rational, with capacity of discernment and response towards our own actions, independent and different. Our personality has its own traits and peculiarities that are created from our personal history and interaction with the environment. Thanks to it, our tastes, needs, priorities and behaviors are defined and maintained in each of the roles and activities we perform in life.

We can find several psychometric instruments that generate complete reports explaining behavioral profiles and levels of emotional intelligence and personality. The most important thing is to be able to interpret the results, to know how it influences in different situations, as well as to consider where we might want to improve and exploit. It is about adapting to the world without losing that which makes us unique.

It is of great importance to invest time in getting to know ourselves and becoming aware of our values, recognizing our potentials, the changes we have and wish to practice, what our motivations and priorities are.

"What you believe in conditions the results you get in life."

By raising our level of consciousness, we take the power of

ourselves to do what truly makes sense to us, aligning goals and objectives with values, which facilitates our path. This begins with small achievements that enhance the connection between our thoughts, emotions and behavior, maintaining a strong motivation. It enables us to accept, exploit and develop new competencies, understand and comprehend what is happening around us, connecting and strengthening interpersonal skills. We assume our responsibility by increasing our commitment to our goals.

In this way, we strengthen our confidence and security, becoming leaders of our own lives, having the conviction that every decision will be made consciously. You will be able to recognize your ability to address current and future challenges. Here, the management of our brand and personal image will be connected with reality and will enable a personal stamp that separates us from others, obtaining an integral and effective growth, understanding the impact we have on the environment to empathize with the world and the people who are part of our trajectory.

The *personal branding* model provides us with a clear structure for each of its phases, designed in such a way that it can be applied to different moments. It is essential to know our beliefs and values, which, during this process, we will learn to use, adapt or modify according to our interests. It mobilizes us to know our real motivations through effective self-knowledge, assuming our potential and strengths. It is necessary to delimit what is important to maintain coherence with ourselves, which will be reflected in the creation of healthy interpersonal bonds to feel internally satisfied and fulfilled as people. This gives us the power to activate a conscious personal commitment, creating our personal brand through an improvement of internal communication, our interrelationships and connection with the context. Thus, we prioritize our well-being and everything we do becomes meaningful, as we gain autonomy, leading our lives with security and confidence.

For the implementation and work of each of the phases, *coaching* and *mentoring* tools and fundamentals are applied, which will be defined below.

Coaching Tools

All of this invites us to believe in ourselves, connecting us with our inner self, establishing as a priority the internal communication to identify and make conscious our values and convictions. It enables the encounter and recognition of our capabilities, resources and potential, leading us to optimize and strengthen them based on our interests, acting to apply them to achieve our goals. We acquire autonomy in our actions, gain confidence and security in ourselves and in our surroundings. We also change our attitudes and interrelationship.

In this methodology of *personal branding*, we will use as a key element the formulation of questions that mobilize us to think beyond what we see at first sight, creating awareness, confidence and clarity of our goals, visualizing more options and motivation to persevere in it. The tools will help us:

- Discover, clarify and define what we want to achieve.
- Promote self-discovery and self-knowledge.
- Encourage the generation of personal solutions and strategies.
- Take personal-responsibility.
- Strengthen our personal commitment.

Mentoring Tools

Mentoring opens up the possibility of co-learning, in which a person with professional and life experience - the mentor - provides the *mentee with* guidance, support and feedback.

Its purpose is to enhance the competencies and skills of the mind through self-knowledge, self-validation and self-awareness, which will improve professional and personal growth to be materialized in concrete results.

Through the *personal branding* model, we will offer guidance in each phase to meet objectives, providing recommendations of tools that we can use to develop personal strategies and meet each proposed goal. If we see the need to replan when we detect the opportunity to deepen a particular topic, we will do it focused in the same direction.

- Strengthens self-responsibility and commitment.
- Planning.
- Advantages of co-learning.
- Identify concrete actions to advance the action plan.
- Support with concrete tools to fulfill commitments and tasks.

Both disciplines provide us with elements that support the basis for the realization of each of the phases of the *personal branding* model. When applying them individually or in the accompaniment of clients, it is essential to recognize from the beginning the values, beliefs, challenges, along with the desired goal. This process is ongoing and requires a high level of commitment.

Now that we are clear on the three dimensions that are part of this model as well as the disciplines that complement them, it is essential to understand that the integral application of the model always goes from the center outward (see figure), to then work through each of the other phases. However, to start your management, you can carry out one of them and then, when you see the need to advance or improve, continue with the others. Be clear that the identification phase is the basis for working on the other six; this is the only one that cannot be missed.

During the following chapters, you will work through each stage. I invite you to dive into them and start managing your personal brand and image to achieve results that positively impact your goals.

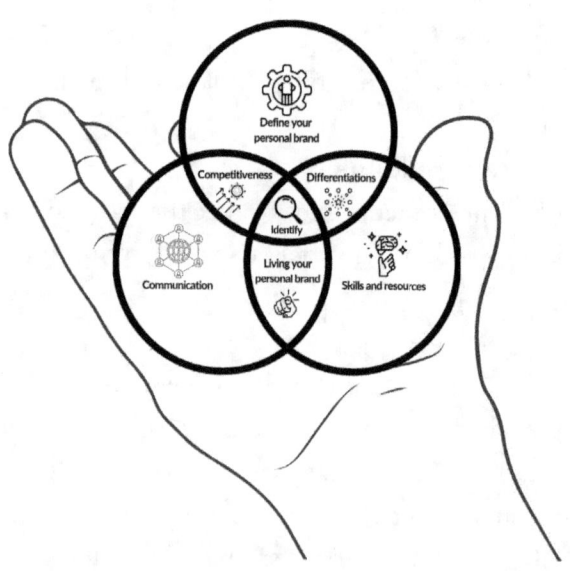

Chapter 1
Identification

Success Starts with You

Let's think of an architectural structure that has to last for many years, where form and space are a set of elements that keep information about other components. This structure must be adapted to manage the climate as well as catastrophes and the demands of the environment, which are often unpredictable.

We begin with the identification phase, understanding our individual needs. This initial step towards our *personal branding* allows us to recognize our beliefs and values, how they influence the way we express and behave as well as the impact they have on our self-concept, our interrelationships and the interaction we have with our environment.

In addition, we will be able to observe the context in which we find ourselves, connecting our inner world with the external world in order to acquire and develop tools to broaden our vision and take charge of managing reality.

It is important to give ourselves the space and time to understand that this phase is a moment of reflection that mobilizes us and provides us with significant aspects to build confidence in ourselves and in what we do.

Beliefs

"I don't have time" "this is not for me" "I am indecisive" "they will say no" "I don't dare" "circumstances won't let me" "I am tired" "I won't be able to" "I don't have enough strength" etc.

Beliefs are powerful messages that our brain receives through physical, psychological, emotional and spiritual experiences. They are installed in us from the first years of life, influenced by the experience of others, our immediate environment and the interactions of the world around us. Their storage affects our perception of ourselves, determining how we interpret and relate to the world.

What supports our beliefs

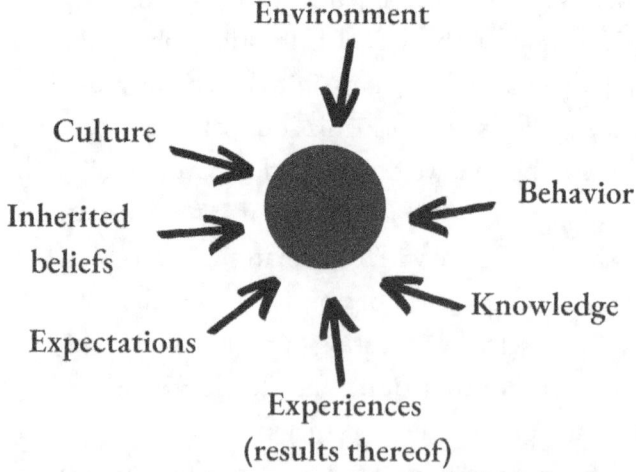

Through this influence, we will shape our behaviors, thoughts, emotions, ideas of success, relationships and the concept of happiness, among others. By building our value system, we form our mental map with generalizations, rules and criteria of limits, capabilities, ideas, behaviors and our own identity.

I invite you to look at the following image and answer: which of the two gray circles is larger?

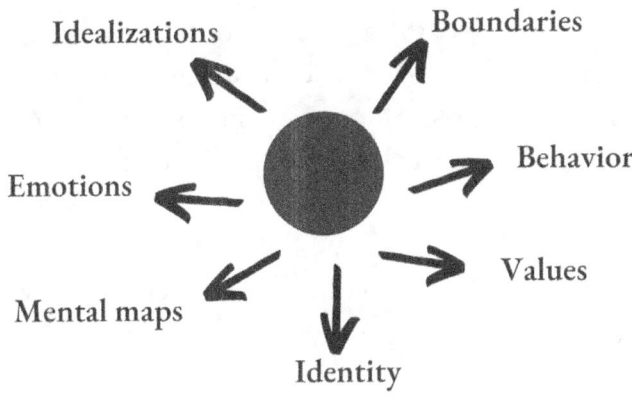

Impact of beliefs

In both images, the gray circles are the same size, only the environment changes, and that makes our perception vary... Incredible!

The mental map we create has an impact on the perception we have of reality, as we see in the previous figure. The meaning we give to situations we encounter in life are interpreted according to our mental map. Thus, as the brain manages an external situation giving it an internal concept that will condition our way of thinking, acting and behaving, in this way, the same reality affects differently in each person, creating multiple actions and decisions, therefore, different results. Two people can observe the same thing and perceive it differently based on their mental map.

By recognizing our mental map, we can seek how to re-signify some perceptions in order to respond better in a particular circumstance. At the same time, by understanding that we each have our own mental map, we broaden the possibility of moving towards a better understanding of the other, positioning ourselves with greater empathy in the face of common experiences.

We can find the appropriate mind maps for each occasion, even combining them appropriately. But we can't take everything we know for granted when we also know other people see and understand things differently. We must consider evidence and why other people see things differently. We should also be open to acquiring new mental models that can be beneficial to us, that help us to broaden our vision and understanding. We do ourselves no favors by refusing new possibilities.

It is essential that we are able to identify the beliefs that we have integrated during life. With a series of questions, we will make this possible. We will help you to refine your vision of what is possible and impossible. We have to consider that our questioning is not directed to classify our convictions as true/false or right/wrong, but to understand if they are limiting or empowering; an essential aspect to keep us motivated to achieve what really makes sense for each person. We then differentiate between two types of beliefs:

> *Limiting:* thoughts that limit us, that prevent us from moving forward. "I am not made for this".
> *Enabling*: those that are pleasant, that invite and motivate us to progress. We take the lead in every action we take. "We don't go backwards or take impulse".

In the following box, we can check the effect that the modification of some limiting beliefs to empowering ones produces in us.

Limiting beliefs	Enabling beliefs
My aspirations are unattainable	By training myself, I will be better prepared to achieve my goals.
I won't have money if I don't sacrifice something	By planning my day, I will be more productive and have time for myself and the people I love.
I have to get it right, I can't fail	I learn from both positive and negative experiences
I have no ability to…	To acquire this skill, I will practice it every day until I achieve it.
I am not as lucky as others	If I put my energy into this, I will succeed.
I was not born to succeed	With hard work and dedication, I will succeed

As we grow up, many of these ingrained limiting beliefs are strengthened, generating an external armor that we believe will help us in our dreams and projects. The influence of this environment sometimes becomes so important that we build our lives based on what others want from us, carrying out our actions with all this information stored in our brain. Without realizing it, we carry an emotional load or a way of seeing life determined by our upbringing and inherited beliefs.

The impact is produced in different areas, creating our reality based on all these convictions that condition the results, often making it more difficult to achieve the desired wellbeing.

Impact of beliefs

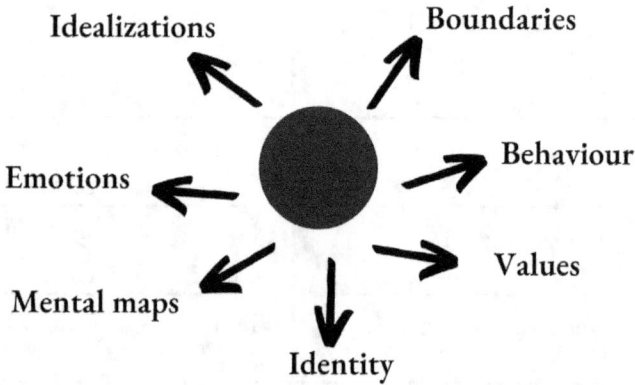

Of all of them, the most powerful are those that influence the formation of the self-concept, because they are the most incorporated in our minds, limiting the possibilities of believing in ourselves and because they define how we perceive ourselves and how we see ourselves in front of the world. When we work on our personal brand and image, we must focus on them in order to modify them positively.

We are responsible for managing our beliefs, with the conviction and sufficient autonomy to trust in what we are and what we long for, using, modifying and building new mental maps that facilitate the path to our achievements.

Values

Loyalty, friendship, love, happiness, empathy, prosperity, gratitude, humility, forgiveness, sincerity, kindness, honesty, respect, tolerance...

As we have seen, convictions modify our value systems, which will be words to which each person attributes a meaning according to the integration of our conscious or unconscious opinions.

Values are essentially our priorities based on beliefs. They are associated with the understanding that every action provokes a reaction and this, in turn, has favorable or less favorable results. They are principles that guide our attitudes and behaviors. They manifest themselves in all contexts of our lives, determining our capacity for tolerance.

Example:

> Value: *loyalty*
> Beliefs:
> "We must always deliver what we have promised."
> "Traitors end up staying alone."
> "You must keep the secrets of others."

There are two types of values, essential and contextual. The former correspond to those that we refuse to change; the latter are those that adapt to the environment in which we find ourselves. Both influence us in provoking the feeling of whether we are doing well or badly.

Each of us subconsciously orders our values based on the degree of importance dependent upon context. They are the engine that drives all our actions and challenges. Thus, in order to remain motivated, it is vital to align behavior or action with values.

The intention in this phase is that we locate the convictions and values, understanding and accepting them. The idea is not to classify them as good or bad, rather, we need to be able to identify which ones will help or hinder us.

Impact of the modification of our beliefs and values

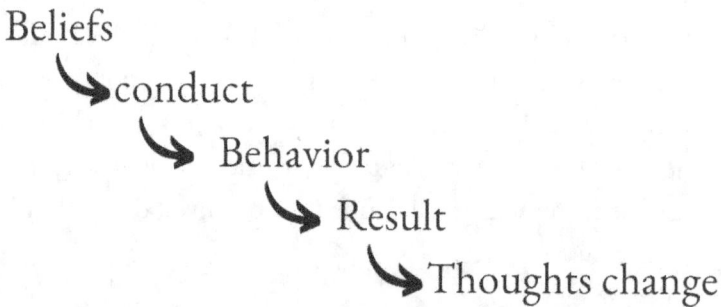

The mind stores information and then uses it automatically when circumstances seem similar, however this isn't always beneficial. The neuroplasticity of our brain allows us to modify and/or adapt the information that has been inherited or acquired. For this to be possible, beliefs must become conscious, making us less resistant to change and growth. I remember the story of a ten-year-old girl who was once asked by her Spanish teacher to get on her chair and recite the vowels. This little girl was so nervous that she couldn't articulate a word. At that moment, the teacher told her, "You will never learn a new language." Since that day, despite her best efforts she has only managed to understand Spanish but cannot speak it. Let us ask this child:

- Why do you think you can't speak another language?
- What could you think of to change that conviction?
- Have you tried standing on a chair and reciting the vowels in Spanish?
- If you try, what do you think will happen?

- And... if you succeed?

Most likely, the moment she tries and realizes that she can, in fact, recite those Spanish vowels, her brain will receive new information that allows her to unblock the original conviction: that she couldn't learn a language. She would receive an enabling message: "I can do it and I did it well."

NLP (neuro-linguistic programming), through studies of human behavior, has focused on understanding these mental and emotional processes, giving us the possibility of understanding how we create and retain these thoughts in our brain. It also provides us with a set of models and techniques to act, think and feel effectively in all areas of existence.

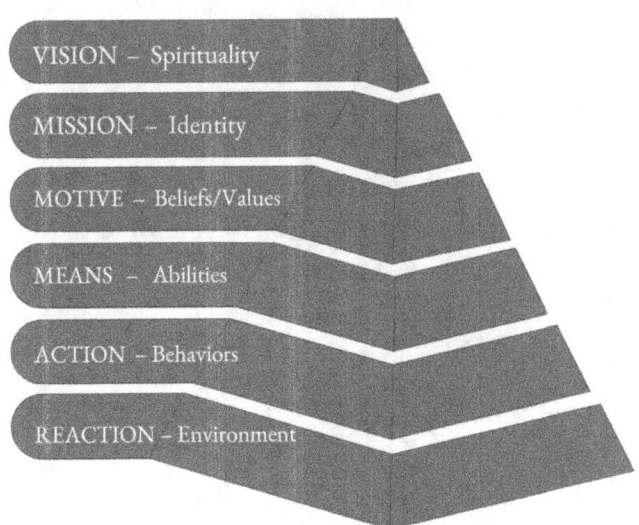

In order to understand behaviors and how to modify them, Robert Dilts, in the 1980s, using the studies of Gregory Bateson, organized them into categories, designing a pyramid of logical levels or Dilts' pyramid, which shows us the levels of how we deal with change, communication and learning procedures.

Thanks to this pyramid, we can see that any variation in a higher level will have an effect on the lower ones. However, a change in a lower level does not necessarily affect the higher ones.

To identify each of the levels, let us ask ourselves the following questions:

- My spiritual and transpersonal dimension: for what or for whom do I do it?
- My identity: Who am I? What am I like? What am I?
- My belief and value system: What motivates me? Why do I do it?
- My capabilities: How? With what?
- My behavior: What do I do?
- My environment: When and with whom?

This hierarchy helps us to visualize at which level our challenge is positioned so that we can act appropriately, organizing our behaviors, understanding that, in order to make a change at any level, we must go to the correct level to achieve the desired results.

A transformation in skills will always bring modifications to our behavior. But if I change my behavior, it does not necessarily affect my skills.

During the pandemic, people became more sensitive to others, but as this was only a change in environment, many lost that sensitivity when they returned to their daily lives. Supermarket cashiers stopped being friendly, some bosses no longer understood the importance of being with family and countless other examples. Even this change was not enough to modify the capacity or ability of empathy. The challenge is to detect at what higher level we are willing to work to enable real behavioral change.

Wheel of Life

Once we are aware of the importance of our values and beliefs, it becomes essential to reflect on our current level of satisfaction in various areas of our lives.

For this there is a *coaching* tool that represents the areas of our life to which we should pay more attention and improve. It was developed by Paul J. Meyer who left us an extensive legacy in leadership, personal achievement and self-improvement. This self-analysis tool, called the Wheel of Life, allows us to evaluate the areas that influence our well-being.

The center of the wheel represents a lower level of satisfaction (0) and the end symbolizes the highest level of satisfaction (10) (example in the image on the right).

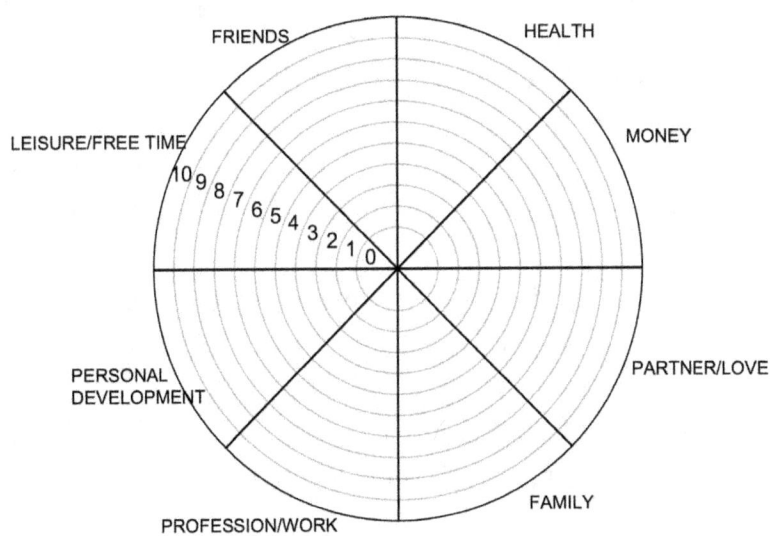

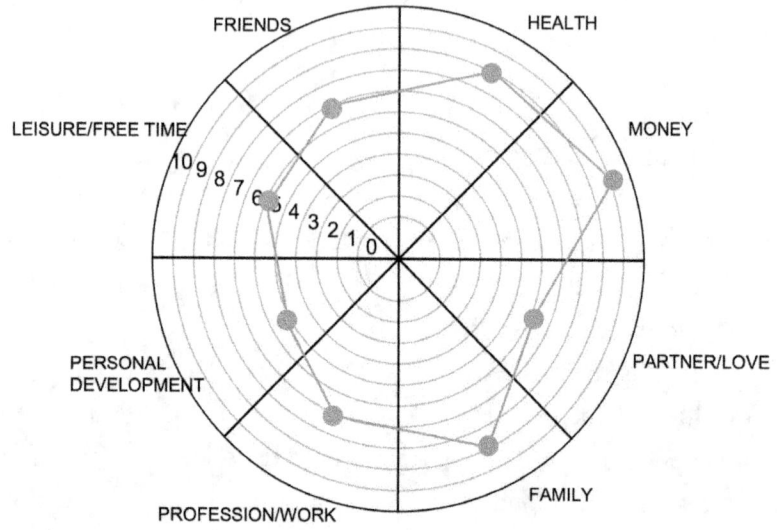

In the image, you can see what is needed to achieve a satisfaction that is as balanced as possible in all areas. This will be our starting point.

During this phase, we have identified our convictions, values, how our thoughts act to produce effective changes and which factors in our life require the most attention at the moment.

This is the most important stage, before we leave our comfort zone and begin to communicate with our inner self to know how we feel and how we want to feel. Here we have space to reflect on what is really valuable, recognizing what we like or dislike about who we are, where are those turning points that will help us to change the results for which we are aiming. From here, a personal strategy is elaborated that facilitates an action plan that goes in the right direction, keeping us motivated.

Here are some questions to review and prepare for the next phase:

Mobilizing Questions

What are my ten values?
_____
_____
_____
_____

Which are the most important?
_____
_____
_____
_____

What objectives are related to your values?
_____
_____
_____
_____

What do you say to yourself when you look in the mirror?
_____
_____
_____
_____

What area of your life is the most important?
___
___
___

What keeps you from moving forward with your projects?
___
___
___

What is getting in your way?
___
___
___

What limitations do you find in yourself?
___
___
___

Chapter 2
Define Your Personal Brand

What Image Do You Want to Build and Project?

Once you have completed phase one, you are able to understand the elements that make up your behaviors, and, in light of this, recognize the way you relate to your surroundings. You are ready to move to the next level. You should always keep in mind that the first phase is the most important of all, it is the core of the model.

As is explained above, *personal branding* is the management of your personal brand: remember that authenticity is one of the most fundamental principles of your brand as you understand that we cannot behave the same way in all contexts.

When developing your brand, keep in mind that it will be visible to others. This is why we manifest what we want to see through our behavior and actions – to ensure we positively impact how we are perceived and remembered. We understand that masks are not effective because at any moment they can drop, leaving us vulnerable in situations where we lack control of our own actions. The elaboration of our personal brand and the projection of this will allow us to project the image we want, delivering to other people a correct and effective message of what we are, creating a unique brand that differentiates us from the rest, through the behavior and the energy we transmit.

In our own way of being, we have to observe what we want to contribute to our environment and where we are going to generate value, maintaining coherence with who we are and what we identify ourselves with. The objective of demonstrating our differences is, of course, highlighting competence in all areas.

To achieve this, in this phase, we will work on knowing our purpose, goal and objectives, so that we draw a plan of action towards the projection of what we really are and want.

We have to consider that many times, in this process, we can lose ourselves, and begin to act in ways that are not true to ourselves. This affects our ability to achieve, not necessarily because of a lack of capacity but due to the lack of coherence between what we ware and what we want.

Purpose

Often, when we hear the word purpose, we ask ourselves endless questions, realizing that we do not have a clear answer. How many times have you regretted not doing something because you did not know where to start? How many times have you chosen another path because you felt you were not competent enough? In our heads, thoughts appear that make us feel disillusioned with ourselves, because, usually, we hear others speak of altruistic purposes or it feels as if our purpose can't be met until some distance future.

Some things I've heard when I ask about purpose:

"My purpose is totally unattainable..." "My venture is my purpose..." "I have a good job, but I can't find my purpose..." "To help people..." "To contribute to underprivileged children..." "Sometimes I don't think I have a purpose..." "I have tried to set one for myself...".

When we talk about purpose, we refer to something intangible and our minds therefore see it as something difficult, for this reason the greatest task is to define it, grounding it to our reality to make it concrete. Having a purpose is what will keep us motivated towards all the goals we set for ourselves, it is what will give meaning to our life making us feel that we are taking advantage of our time to contribute to our world.

Experience has shown me that when we set a goal, it is often associated with wanting to give something valuable to a person, family, community, society and even the world. There is some degree of satisfaction, to contributing in our own small way, to making the planet a better place. This has made me realize that the common good is the principle that governs what we yearn for, perhaps because we are certain that our security and confidence also depend on the environment.

The purpose must make sense to us, we must be one hundred percent aware of what we want so that it develops, takes shape and becomes concrete. We must be careful that does not remain just an idea.

The first step is to accept the challenge and understand that the current state in which we find ourselves is an opportunity to harvest what we long for. It is not about going from point A to point B magically. It is important to understand that, in order to achieve the objective starting at A, we have to set several goals that will allow us to go step by step to point B. When we see that we can achieve "small" goals, we will feel more motivated to continue with the following ones until we reach our final, overarching goal.

We live in constant movement, so our purpose is not static; rather, it changes and evolves with us. It is essential that it be coherent with our genuine values and aspirations, taking care that they are neither too high nor too low so that we do not feel disappointed when we see that we cannot move towards it or that it is meaningless.

To facilitate your purpose statement, I suggest that you make a list by answering the following questions, each one of them in order of importance to you:

- What is your favorite thing to do?
- What are you good at?
- What activities or environments make you feel good and happy?
- If you had more free time, where would you spend it?
- What do you want most in your life?
- What do you want to achieve it for?

Choose the most important one and consider what you need to do to achieve it, find the smaller goals that will help you reach it.

From time to time, we will inquire into the same questions to take a direction that will allow us to visualize small goals and, thus, fulfill the purpose we long for. To do this, we will always look for a comfortable and quiet place where we can answer each of the questions, giving ourselves time to reflect, avoiding the fear of the challenge to cloud our minds. When we learned to walk, there was no fear, because there was no more information in our brain; let's remember that we are the owners of our thoughts. We will visualize our closest desire and this will be the beginning of our journey.

This is an invitation to action, not to wait until we have all the elements to achieve our purpose, but rather, with the resources we have and the opportunities we have, to start on this journey.

"To stay motivated, we must set ourselves challenges in life."

Goals

To some extent, we all seek to progress in life by channeling our energies towards achieving results. Setting a purpose alone will not be satisfactory if we do not have the desired success, that is why it is important to set clear goals. Personal success is perceived by our mind as we see that we are progressing.

Our goals must be consistent with what makes sense to us and with our values. In turn, they must be established by classifying them according to the different areas of our life.

When setting our goals, we will consider the following factors:

Be measurable.

Be achievable.

Be clear.

Be specific.

Classified in short, medium and long term.

There are several methods of to do this. Depending on the image of our company or even our own image, we will select the correct method. Some will focus on work teams or personal development and others on the welfare of the planet. The method we choose has to be consistent with what we have set as our purpose.

In this *personal branding* model, for the definition of our goals, we will use the SMART method designed by George T. Doran, who, in the eighties, published in the *Management Review Magazine*, a *paper* called "There's a S.M.A.R.T. Way to Write Management's Goals and Objectives." There he defined the five characteristics that should be considered when setting goals. The method allows you to easily identify both personal and professional goals.

SMART METHOD		
S Specific	Your goal should be clear and well defined. If it is very general, break it down into several smaller ones and focus on one at a time.	What do you want to do? What do you want?
M Measurable	That it is quantifiable in order to know the degree of progress. Define dates, percentages, etc. When the objective is clear, it can be easily measured.	How much? How will you know that you reached it? What is the unit with which I am going to measure it?
A Attainable or Achievable	It helps you to set another goal and move on. Match the challenge to the skills, abilities and resources you have. There must be a balance. In your current circumstances, you can fulfill it.	How? Is it in ourselves to achieve it? Do we have the skills, abilities and resources? Can we acquire them? Where are our limits?
R Relevant	The positive impact it has on your life, profession and/or entrepreneurship. It has to arouse motivation.	What for? Is it possible to achieve it? Is it important to me? What would happen if you gave up that goal? Will it deliver any real satisfaction?
T Timely	Define when you want it to take place by setting a time limit.	When? What is the deadline?

Once we have defined our goals, we must give priority to the most important one, focusing our energies to avoid changing it or modifying it halfway through. The idea is to achieve it while enjoying the process you need to carry it out. The achievement of each of these small goals will allow us to generate better results and optimize our time, which will make us feel more satisfied and motivated to see that we are contributing every day to our purpose.

For each goal, we must establish the stages defining the concrete actions we will take to achieve it, this will provide us with clarity in our progress.

When we maintain satisfaction, we feel that every progress is due to perseverance and personal motivation.

Action Plan

We know our current situation, we have projected our goals, objectives and purposes, and now it is time to design our action plan. In other words, we know that we are at the edge of the ocean that we must navigate, we know our point of arrival, now we must plan our journey.

When we know the path, we will build a plan that clearly defines the steps to be taken. The design of our action plan will have to be based on our commitment, dedication and perseverance. By achieving each step, we will feel confident and secure, which will provide us with greater motivation.

Action plan design

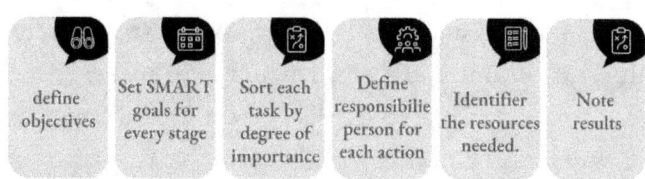

Important points to consider:

- Set the start and end date.
- Count how much time you have.
- Divide the time into stages. E.g., each stage lasts two days.
- Define the number of stages.
- For each stage, define milestones.
- Set your goal.
- Define objectives by stage and actions to be carried out.

Then, for each stage:

- Check what resources you require. How can you acquire them?
- Define which activities depend on you and which involve third parties.
- In activities involving third parties, what role do they play?
- Is it feasible?
- Establish a measure for each progress.
- Review what could impede development and compliance.
- What will be the measures and actions that should be taken

if it is not complied with? Do you have a Plan B?

Results

Once you start executing your action plan, check your progress using the PDCA model The PDCA model was designed by Walter Andrew Shewhart, an American physicist and pioneer in quality control. It was later popularized in the 1950s by Edward Deming, a professor known for his contribution to improving production procedures in the U.S. during World War II and also for his consulting work with Japanese executives. The PDCA cycle or Deming cycle is used for continuous improvement. It is a tool that helps us to optimize and facilitate the effectiveness of our action plan through these four stages, which you will then evaluate.

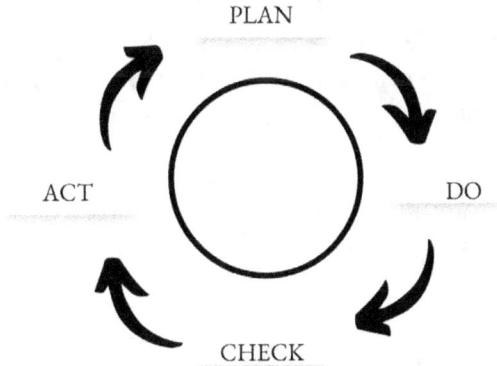

Below, we can see how to apply it:

Plan: the first step is to have our planning prepared, defining the objectives and activities to be carried out.

What is our goal?
What are our goals?
How will we do it?

Do: we start executing our planning, reviewing: what problems do we face in executing the planning? What is most effective?

Check: we will review the results against the expected results in each of the stages before moving on to the next stage.

What made it difficult for us to obtain the results? What made it possible?

Act: if the results are satisfactory, we continue to the next stage and, if not, we must review what we will change to achieve it.

What was the reason for not complying with this stage of the plan?

What needs to be changed to comply?

Once the last stage is finished, we must go back to the first stage and repeat the cycle again, it is a constant process with which we will improve each time.

To maintain momentum and enthusiasm, we need to be motivated, remember this is the engine that will move you to develop the tasks and activities proposed in your personal planning. Therefore, we must reflect on how we have made the changes and what we are learning from each other, acquiring a personal commitment to progress in our action plan, getting closer to our purpose every day.

Personal Image

Defining our purpose, goals and establishing a plan of action, makes us recognize in ourselves the true engine that moves our lives. However, we often fail to let our environment know our true motivations. This can work against us when our image conveys a message that is totally different from what we are. Even if we want to go unnoticed, our image speaks clearly of who we are, what we want, our values and how we want to be considered.

We all have a personal image, but not all of us have worked on it to build a personal brand. Those who have deliberately built their personal brand have standing out, being more competitive and of feeling more secure and confident.

Today, we are part of a globalized society, which means that success does not depend on your skills alone. Your appearance plays a key role in reflecting your intentions and the value you bring.

Think of a specific item of clothing. How did you feel when you wore it? At this moment, memories should come to your mind where you are filled with feelings of satisfaction, security, power or perhaps sadness, fear or nervousness. This is called *enclothed cognition*. In 2012, Hajo Adam and Adam Galinsky, from Northwestern University in the USA, coined this term that defines the systematic influence that clothing has on cognitive processes where two independent factors are mixed: the symbolic meaning that our way of dressing has and the physical experience of wearing it. For example, wearing pajamas at home makes you feel relaxed and can even make you feel sleepy, so I do not recommend it when you work at home, as your concentration will inevitably decrease.

For this reason, in order to achieve an integral result of our personal image, paying attention to the way we dress will be key to project what we want to achieve.

In constructing our personal image, we will consider four essential factors: behavior, appearance, nonverbal communication and attitude. In the previous chapter, we identified the elements that determine our behavior; in chapter six, we will review nonverbal language, and, in this chapter, we will address appearance and attitude.

Appearance

Personal care: an impeccable physical appearance reveals our personal value. We must not neglect our hygiene, even if we are already known, we must always maintain coherence. A messy bedroom or desk shows how your mind is. Be careful not to ignore those messages that our brain and the brains of those around us are receiving.

Style: defining it will be an important part to feeling confident in our image. When you define your style, you have clarity of colors, prints, types of clothing and accessories, through which we produce coherence of what others see with who we are.

There are seven universal styles:

Natural style: what stands out in this style is the practicality and simplicity in everyday life. People who dress this way enjoy the small details of life. They look for comfort, durable garments and easy maintenance.

Romantic style: those who dress in this style stand out for their warmth and sensitivity. They care about aesthetics and beauty in all areas of their lives. They prefer to dress in soft and drapey fabrics.

Dramatic style: there is a suggestion of impulsiveness, of giving in to whims, the dramatic dressers stand out for their sophistication and avant-garde personalities. People with this style are attracted to intense and fashionable colors.

Classical/traditional style: suggests a need for order and rules. Responsibility and loyalty are priorities. Preference for classic clothes, with straight cuts and traditional fabrics. They are attracted to fine jewelry.

Sensual style: people who express emotions in a confident manner. They live with intensity. They value self-care and aesthetics. They like to dress attractively with intense colors and clothes that make them stand out from others.

Creative style: for those who express their differences with confidence, authenticity and originality. They are attracted to original clothing, colors and contrasts.

Elegant style: respect, culture and refinement are the basis of their life. They stand out for projecting in a distinguished way their personal security. They seek to dress with perfect fit. They are concerned that every detail is in place.

Which style do you identify with?

Dress code: each culture has its own dress code, so we are responsible for knowing it before attending a ceremony, event or meeting. Respect for a host is shown in the way we dress.

How would you feel if your dinner guest arrived with unkempt clothing or dirty hands?

Color psychology: colors play an important role in our appearance. They stimulate emotions in our surroundings and in us, influencing decision making and behavior.

Each color, culturally, has a meaning that provides information about us and can even influence how much we are remembered. Thus, it is an important factor in projecting what we want and who we are.

Have you noticed that, in spring, when all the gardens are full of color, you are in better spirits?

Choosing the right colors will be an advantage in our appearance, do not forget the context and remember to consider the colors that best suit you when choosing your wardrobe, makeup and environment.

Below I share the meaning of some colors:

Yellow: denotes optimism, friendliness, positivity, energy, joy, warmth, fun, youthfulness, creativity, intelligence, caution, instability.

Orange: innovation, modernity, youth, fun, friendship, enthusiasm, action, happiness, accessibility, courage, energy, vitality, ambition.

Red: dynamism, revolution, energy, power, strength, passion, love, heat, hunger, ambition, risk, danger, anger.

Pink: fun, sensitivity, compassion, delicacy, femininity, friendship, passion, creativity, sweetness, innocence, immaturity.

Purple: success, ambition, intuition, wisdom, sophistication, royalty, dignity, serenity, creativity, imagination, abundance, power, extravagance, luxury, distinction, mystery, spirituality.

Blue: professionalism, seriousness, integrity, sincerity, health, calm, security, productivity, intelligence, confidence, imagination, strength, harmony.

Green: growth, serenity, nature, ecology, freshness, health, fertility, hope, positivity, growth, balance, stability, peace, youth.

Brown: simplicity, nature, comfort, warmth, stability, confidence, efficiency, professionalism, quality, maturity.

Black: value, prestige, elegance, authority, power, luxury, sophistication, mystery, formality, timelessness, exclusivity, sensuality, security.

White: purity, peace, clarity, elegance, innocence, perfection, order, cleanliness, simplicity, softness, freshness.

Gray: opacity, authority, simplicity, respect, neutrality, humility.

Attitude

As Victor Küppers rightly says, "no one will remember you for your resume, but for the way you are."

Life is full of decisions and one of the most important is

to decide how we are going to face each of the challenges that arise. We must assume our responsibility in every situation and experience.

Every time I start a talk, I ask my audience: how are you feeling today? There is an incredible variety of responses, feelings of anticipation, joy, sadness or loneliness. As I review their responses, I find that many people have a way of feeling that leads them to have a more positive attitude while others are mired in disappointment or sadness. In a way, this question leads you to put yourself in the center and understand that it is up to you to make the most of it. Then I ask those who have negative feelings to tell the feelings to get out of their head, to wait there for a moment until the end of the talk, that they aren't needed now. At the end, I encourage them to talk to the feeling they had at the beginning and tell it that it can come in, that's when the "magic" happens, they can't find it, it's gone! What happened? The attitude changed.

Attitude is a state of mind that depends on values and beliefs, which provoke certain emotions in different situations based on the context in which we find ourselves. That is why it is important to work on our self-knowledge, to find what elements are impacting our attitude towards life. There are more difficult moments, but be sure that how you face that circumstance, the decision you make, and your behavior will depend on your attitude.

You will tell me that it is easy to say when you are on the other side of the street, but who else can understand the situation than yourself. No one can truly put themselves in your shoes, they can be empathetic, but that doesn't mean the other person can even get close to understanding what is really going on with you.

So, what do we do? Use your positive thoughts, look for opportunities to learn from each juncture and draw energy to continue. Seek to transform that moment in your favor or adapt to it in pursuit of your personal growth. This is the hardest thing to do because it takes us out of our comfort zone. However, no matter what, the reality is that everything depends on you. Now, what attitude are you going to take?

During this phase of the *personal branding* model, we recognize and become aware of each of the elements described to find, define and build our personal brand, which allows us to manage it consciously.

We must always maintain a real commitment that, in addition to responsibility and discipline, contains passion towards the objectives set. Through this model, we will generate awareness of how important it is for each of us to fulfill our personal agreements as well as those acquired with others. By connecting with our individual purpose, our contribution will be more integral in all areas.

Now, consider and answer the questions below in order to really integrate the key points of this chapter into your thinking:

Mobilizing Questions

What is your dream?
_____
_____
_____

What footprint do you want to leave?
_____
_____

What is most important to you?

_____
_____
_____
_____

What moments have been valuable to you?

_____
_____
_____
_____

How would you show your gratitude?

_____
_____
_____
_____

What makes you passionate about this purpose?

_____
_____
_____
_____

What topics are interesting to you?

_____
_____
_____
_____

How will you feel about achieving your goals?

_____
_____

What is getting in the way?

Is your life going the way you want it to?

What do you want to achieve?

How do you want to do it?

Chapter 3
Skills and Resources

Supporting Your Personal Brand

Another of the principles of *personal branding* is based on generating awareness of who we are, what we want and our impact on others. Knowing ourselves and recognizing ourselves promotes personal value, awakening our self-esteem and affecting our self-concept. The latter is essential for us to feel capable of facing the challenges that come our way.

Many of us have grown personally and professionally under the gaze of others who test our abilities and skills, which can cause insecurity. Sometimes we are even evaluated in things in which we are not skilled or, simply, in things that do not go with our way of being. By this, I mean, for example, that introverts may find it more difficult to speak publicly so should not feel frustrated when it doesn't go well – instead perhaps they are the people who could write the speeches.

This does not mean that the doors are closed there, because if it is important to us, we have to work to develop habits that allow us to obtain these skills. Internal communication plays a key role in the intrapersonal path, enabling us to accept and understand ourselves. Internal communication is another principle of this *personal branding* model.

Self-knowledge gives us the opportunity to balance our aptitudes with our interests. Thus, when faced with any obstacle, we will find more options and opportunities to overcome it, being able to manage our talents and bringing with it an increase in our security, self-confidence and self-motivation.

We all have different characteristics and skills that make up our personal brand, with more or fewer points of attraction. We are all different and in these particularities lies the value of each one of us.

It is our responsibility to create a commitment to continuous improvement, advancing in the management of our personal brand.

Skills

Each of us possesses a set of skills, whether innate, acquired from childhood or through experience, areas of interest and objectives. The ones we focus on most in depth at each stage of the model will be those that facilitate our goals.

Skills are grouped into two types, soft skills and hard skills. The latter are acquired through experience, education and technical knowledge. On the other hand, soft skills are those that are transferable to any field, they are both interpersonal and social.

Both types of skill can be acquired or enhanced through the formation of new habits, knowledge, practice and training. The greater and more effective use of this set of skills will depend on personal commitment.

Soft (social) skills	Hard skills (knowledge)
Adaptability	
Communication	Engineering
Conflict resolution	Mathematics
Creativity	Data analysis
Decision making	Foreign language fluency
Leadership	Design
Motivation	Technology
Teamwork	*Marketing*, among others
Time management, among others	

The *personal branding* model focuses mainly on finding and recognizing soft skills, which, depending on our own interests and needs, are enhanced throughout the process. This does not mean that other skills are not important in the achievement of our objectives; rather, these are the ones that support the professional development that, together with the soft skills, make us more competitive.

Generally, it is difficult for us to identify soft skills, since they are not visible to the naked eye, adding to that being inserted in a society where the negative is highlighted more than the positive. Thus, pointing them out will require time to reflect and improve our self-knowledge, giving room for internal communication to self-evaluate. To take the first step, we should ask ourselves the following questions:

- What do you like to do and what do you find easy?
- What do other people highlight about you?
- What skills have helped you achieve success?
- In what environments do you feel most confident? What skills do you use?
- What qualities stand out in your personality?
- What skills would you like to have?

Soft skills will be, therefore, those belonging to the social sphere, marking how we relate to others, directly impacting our results and achievements in any area of our lives. Recognizing and enhancing them makes it easier for us to detect those we need to acquire and improve, making it possible to manage and use them effectively and efficiently, leading the way to achieving our goals.

Their development depends on our level of self-knowledge, self-awareness, the formation of habits, the generation of virtuous bonds and the value provided by the environment. For some, it may be easier than for others, so we must remain honest with ourselves and evaluate the possibility of support through a mentor, *coach* or a professional who works in these areas.

FOAR Tool

In the *personal branding* model, we will use SOAR, an analysis tool created by David L. Cooperrider. This is based on appreciative inquiry (AI), where the focus is on the positive and constructive aspects of each of us, approaching the results from an enabling perspective. Through the analysis of strengths and opportunities, we concretize aspirations and commitment to achieve the expected results, that is, aimed at improving our personal strategies.

Strengths

An internal analysis of our present strengths as natural ability that has the characteristic of being good in itself. It can be developed, it is measurable and malleable. It is what we use when we achieve the results we aspire to.
- What are you good at?
- What do you excel at?

- What do you like most about yourself?

Confidence, resilience, courage, empathy, effective communication, active listening, sensitivity, logic, intuition, patience, leadership, motivation, commitment, decisiveness, responsibility, etc.

Opportunities

An external analysis of any situation or positive factor that occurs in the environment and that can be used to originate our own benefits, which put us at an advantage for the achievement of our goals. Here we also consider which skills that we can improve and that, in some way, by doing so, we can perceive opportunity.
- What areas can you strengthen and enhance?
- What can you use to your advantage?
- What personal and professional networks, environment and experience do you have?

Profession, family, social environment, friends, *networking*, personal resources, knowledge, skills, etc.

Aspiration

A personal internal analysis, it is what we strongly desire, that which motivates us is based on what interests us, what we like and what we are passionate about.
- What do you want to be in the future?
- How do you want to be in the future?
- What do you strongly desire?

Studying another language, healthy eating, losing weight, improving my relationship with my children, starting my own business, getting a high position in my job, etc.

Results

An analysis of the future, the final effects of all the actions we take. These results must be clear and focused to achieve our goal. They must be measurable and quantifiable.
- What are the measurable results you want to achieve?
- How will you know you made it?
- How will you highlight your strengths?

Speaking another language, improving my glycemic index, losing five kilos, creating a space for conversation with my children every Friday, registering my company in two months, becoming a manager, etc.

This is how the perceptions we held at the beginning of this chapter have totally changes to how we view things now, our minds are opening to new possibilities and options for us to reach our purpose. See, our purpose is not as far off as we thought.

Even so, there is something we are missing so that we can really feel that we have what we need.

Resources

Recognizing our skills and strengths, that is, the personal resources we have, we must also keep in mind the material instruments we have available and define which are the ones we need to advance in each of the stages, goals and objectives set forth in our action plan.

Material resources are physical and tangible means. For example: computer, internet, financial capacity, tools, infrastructure and inputs.

As we can see, each person possesses natural qualities and abilities, personal and material resources that can often be very similar to each other, but the big difference will be in identifying them, developing them, acquiring them and enhancing them, thus creating a personal strategy to optimize personal results.

The management of all these elements allows us to size the adjustments we have to make in order to make each of them available, using them efficiently and effectively and studying, with clarity, what we are missing.

"The best skill is to focus on our strengths to maintain motivation."

The following are some questions to help you review the information in this chapter.

Mobilizing Questions

What successful situations do you remember?
___
___
___

What did you do to achieve this?
___
___
___

What quality do you recognize in that situation?
___
___
___

What would you have done differently?

What did you like about yourself at that moment?

What do you take away from that experience?

Chapter 4
Differentiation

What Makes You More Visible?

In this phase, we will work from the basis of the concept of uniqueness, understanding that every person is unique, unrepeatable and irreplaceable. Among the ten principles of *personal branding* is differentiation.

The concept of differentiation is very valuable at all stages of our lives, understanding that, although we are inserted in society belonging to a group of people with norms, values and customs, we will always retain particularities that make us unique. Even so, we have very little awareness of the real importance that this differentiation has in practice. If we take it back to our childhood, little or nothing educates us in the self-knowledge and signaling of our differences as part of our strengths, rather, weaknesses and the achievement of results according to the expectations of the environment, measured with the experiences of others, are highlighted. For this reason, we have to consider that many of our strengths are invisible to our own eyes, which generates insecurity and distrust. It is not so strange then that this leads us down the path of least resistance, which is to imitate others, losing the most important element of our existence: uniqueness.

Naturally, as we grow up, we see the need to differentiate ourselves from others, feeling more responsible for building our personality based on our way of thinking, feeling and understanding of life. Thus, we begin to select which external messages we receive, picking up what makes sense to us. As beings inserted in a society, we build our identity day by day by adding behaviors, expectations, ideas, beliefs and behavior patterns since childhood. Our social and family environment provides us with messages that influence our structure of thought and behavior, these messages show us what is right and what is wrong, assimilating and integrating each one of them without necessarily having a formed personal criterion.

In this journey, in addition to what we select, we incorporate what is "good" for other people, burdening ourselves with expectations of what they expect from us, without taking into account our perspective, making others' thoughts our own and losing control of our life and power over ourselves.

"Love yourself as you are."

For this reason, it is crucial to review which of these messages, thoughts and behaviors are contributing to enhance our particularities, detecting those that we must begin to cement through new learning, those that we have to enhance or modify to promote our differentiating elements, strengthening our personal brand to transcend at any point.

In order to differentiate ourselves, we will focus on these six elements and then move on to action with the development of our value proposition.

1. Authenticity

The differentiation strategy in the *personal branding* model prioritizes the highlighting of our personal brand through authenticity, which is reflected in the coherence and impact of what we are and what we do. This, coupled with how we are perceived by others, while maintaining the focus on our talent and capabilities, our environment, our particularities and the contribution of value is relevant. In this sense, we must be careful not to fall into mediocrity in the search for perfection, in other words, not to settle for what there is or to persist in complying with pre-established canons by the environment in which we operate. It is fundamental to establish a balance between what we are and what we can deliver, which is produced through self-knowledge, where we recognize our particularities, expanding the range of possibilities and opportunities for improvement, reaffirming self-acceptance and self-management.

"You are a great person, stop for a moment and focus on you."

The best way to know is to connect with ourselves and communicate with our inner selves, searching for our true identity without masks and resorting to the questions we once had to answer in philosophy classes; who am I, what defines me, where am I going?

The responsibility of our behaviors is an important part of being authentic, this is where our true self is shown. Our personality and emotions are revealed in them. The essential thing is to be consistent with ourselves by putting who we are first, defending what makes us feel good and what does not, showing integrity, respect and empathy to others. This will show in our actions, which will speak of our personality, what we think and what we do, even if no one is watching us.

Our personality, as we have already seen, defines us by

means of our own characteristics that distinguish us from other people and by which we are known. We can have the same personality, skills and qualities as other people, but, however, what will make the difference is how we interpret and react to situations, highlighting our particular behavior and the way we communicate to connect with others. This will undoubtedly be a great advantage when it comes to relating to others, which will open up a world of possibilities.

We should not be afraid of rejection; let us remember that, in these differences, lies our true self-identity.

When we are authentic, we are confident in our abilities, leaving out complexes and fears, increasing our self-esteem, we make good decisions and, in this way, we will be identified as credible and trustworthy people. This is a great differentiating element.

We must not lose sight of the great enemies of being truly authentic: lack of credibility, lack of confidence in our own abilities, not being who we are, not doing what we want to do, making decisions influenced by others, vulnerability and loss of our autonomy.

2. Passion

It is a factor that you cannot leave out, it is the fuel for you to move every day, the one that makes you get up with enthusiasm and overcome difficulties with a more enabling look.

We must be careful how we understand passion, we have been formed believe that you find it when you leave that "boring job" or "when you are your own boss." We see images on social networks that show us digital nomads sitting on a perfect beach, cocktail in hand still earning money with the caption: "Find your passion." We know well that this leads to frustration with our own situation. But remember, they are selling us the idea of lifestyle rather than true passion.

Passion is not so far from reality. Indeed, the feeling of true passion for life is as pleasant as being on the beach. And don't forget that on that wonderful beach there are often unseen complications that challenge us: wind, hurricanes, hot weather, sand on our towel, sunstroke, etc.

To recognize passion, it is important to keep in mind that it is the fuel for motivation and gives you personal satisfaction. Search then, what do you love, what are you good at, what gives you motivation, what inspires you, what do you enjoy doing, what are you excited about doing?

Passion should be sought in the things we do every day: in work, activities, sports and hobbies. The difference to note is that passion is, above all, what we do constantly, to which we dedicate most of our physical and mental time, where we put all our personal and material resources.

This is how we can say that passion is made up of smaller passions that keep us motivated to do things that sometimes we don't enjoy very much, but that give us what we need to fulfill that passion. We can have passion for what we do, for what our tasks let us do or for the reason behind what we do. So, when we seek our passion, let us immediately think that it is not about changing everything we do, but about directing those efforts towards what we are passionate about. In this way, we will feel great satisfaction.

We can have a job that we may not like so much, but that, by earning resources through it, allows us to perform an activity that we are passionate about, such as taking a perfect vacation in the Caribbean. A very clear example is the one we see in the movie *The Pursuit of Happiness*, where the character played by

Will Smith is shown as a passionate father who strives to provide a better life for his son. That keeps him motivated to pursue that job and fulfill his passion.

We must be careful with those *hobbies* disguised as passion, remember that this is constant and is what fuels our motivation. A hobby can be intellectual or practical, where we seek a space of distraction or a way to entertain us, it helps us to spread our mind and relax, unlike our passion, it demands less amount of time. With this I do not mean that it is bad, on the contrary, a hobby helps to exercise the body and mind, with it we can develop other disciplines, relieve tensions, diversify our social life, among other things. Rather, we have to visualize the difference when we define our passion.

3. Life History

Telling your story is an excellent tool for successful differentiation.

Being authentic and identifying our passion is the first step to build a personal *storytelling* focused on who we are, based on our own life experience and what elements make us stand out from others. The idea is that, through this, we deliver to the other an invitation to know these elements that have led us to be what we are today.

Regardless of the roles we play, our personal history will always contain experiences that we can share with others in order to provide them with elements that help them to visualize more options from their own point of view and relating to their own situation. Therefore, they will perceive us as authentic and supportive people. This will set you apart from the rest.

4. How You Communicate

Communication is a differentiating element that is present at all times. We are constantly communicating through our gestures, voice, attitude, emotions, behavior, etc. Therefore, we will be distinguished and remembered by people according to the interaction that is established and the bonds that we generate through that communication. Building these bridges gives us a great value when it comes to setting ourselves apart from others.

One simple way to make and maintain ties is to address people by name. This helps to break the ice, connecting us with the other, transmitting that the person is important to us, facilitating the understanding and the predisposition to a communication with better connection. Sometimes, it can be difficult to remember the name, a trick that can help us is to relate the person with a particular characteristic, so our brain integrates it more easily. An example of this could be: "Andrea is the one who always has a cup of coffee."

Another resource is to inform ourselves about who we are communicating with and the context in which we find ourselves, modeling the message so that it is understandable and clear, using the right words at the right time, connecting with people with a language that is simple enough to be transferred and interpreted correctly.

It is important to emphasize that it is the attitude that builds this bridge and that it depends not only on the person who transfers it, but also on the person who receives it. Later on, we will detail the elements that are important to consider for an effective communication.

For now, it is important to understand that the intention of working on the way you communicate is to make yourself visible through effective, sincere and empathetic communication, which will open the doors to the creation of real bonds that make a difference.

5. Never Stop Learning

Experience, acquiring knowledge to deliver the best of you, is part of keeping yourself current and informed. The biggest challenge is to reinvent yourself from the value you can deliver, for this reason it is of great importance to be visionary and creative.

Although we all have certain capabilities and elements that are central to our differentiation, it is important to diversify them in order to enrich our competencies, without forgetting that we are the basis of everything and that we require a regular effort of self-knowledge.

When we need to adapt to change, we can see it as an opportunity to develop in other areas rather than perceive defeat. Of course, the only way that will lead us to think this way is to be clear about our skills and resources, making it very important to periodically review your "tool kit" to use them.

Learning expands your options and vision regarding the possible opportunities that lie behind those changes or challenges that arise. Many times, we forget how important learning is to modify and acquire knowledge and behaviors that lead us to be flexible and adaptable to different situations, and of course, both are qualities that will differentiate you from others.

6. Self-care

Finding spaces to feel relaxed and connect with ourselves to facilitate our internal communication makes it easier to visualize areas that we need to strengthen for the different activities we perform. By valuing both the personal characteristics that are strengths and those that we need to acquire, it impacts on the self-esteem that builds our well-being. It changes our perception of ourselves and the world around us, increasing self-esteem and self-concept, which we will show through our behaviors and emotions.

Self-care is an element that we must not lose sight of. When we seek to differentiate ourselves, this element is essential to gain the trust of others and to be perceived with certainty about what we are and what we do.

This is where our *hobbies* come in, they are the best ally against depression, anxiety, nervousness, as well as helping to prevent diseases such as Alzheimer's – dancing, gardening, playing cards, playing an instrument, are all good options.

"Your habits reflect your self-care."

Reflect by answering the following questions:

- How much time do you dedicate to yourself?
- Do you think about what people will say?
- How critical are you of yourself?
- When will you start worrying about your well-being?

From Idea to Action

The set of competencies and skills that we detect in ourselves will enable us to objectively and clearly evaluate the differentiating elements, locating the advantages based on each context. These elements must be connected to us and in this case, they are our values, our passion, our life story, our way of communicating and experiences. This is how we will be strengthening the authenticity of our personal brand.

The identification of differentiating elements makes it easier for us to distinguish the real contribution we are making and makes us more visible. When our contribution is authentically connected to us, the environment perceives it by recognizing in us that differentiating element. In the same way, we then find the true meaning of our actions, which gives us greater personal satisfaction, influencing our motivation which, in turn, is directly related to making better decisions and, consequently, to the achievement of our well-being, which leverages our results.

Value	Personal qualities	What makes you different?	What do you like to do (that is in line with the value you registered)?
Loyalty	High commitment	Perform my duties on time	I like to be accountable
Leadership	I keep order	I am capable of distributing and organizing the tasks of a work team.	I would like to have my own business

To find these elements, I invite you to fill out the following table, reflecting and answering the questions raised. Use the ten values you described in chapter 1.

As we can see, sometimes we do not perceive our qualities, because we find them so obvious and easy that they seem insignificant. But really, these are the ones that make us more visible and given us a comparative advantage, differentiating us in our personal, social, work environment or in our company brand. The main reason why we struggle to find that distinction is because we are looking for that unique element that others do not have, when, in fact, it may be the same thing that others have, but it is based on our own history and experience, it is the essence of what we deliver authentically.

When we find these differentiators, we are prepared so that, in whatever role we play in life, we are more adept at detecting, developing and delivering what they need and, thus, have the ability to do something better or different than others.

Value Proposition

We are now ready and on track to build the value proposition based on our own story together with our authentic characteristics, which are communicated to our environment activating a kind of magnet that attracts people's interest in us.

Both individuals and companies look for characteristics in others that lead to the resolution of problems, that provide security, stability and commitment in the work they perform.

To elaborate a personal or focused value proposition for a client, company or employer, it is essential to make one for each, identifying unique characteristics, looking for the qualities in us that generate value for them as well as for us and our learning to mobilize us focused on strengthening, activating and adapting our hard and soft skills, managing them according to our objectives.

A tool that I use in my sessions and that facilitates the development of a value proposition for professionals, entrepreneurs, companies, products and services is the Canvas model value proposition canvas, written by Alex Osterwalder, Ives Pigneur, Greg Bernarda and Alan Smith. In this canvas, through a clear methodology, it step by step creates a segmented value proposition that defines what you offer as value so that you deliver the expected results and benefits.

To start filling out the canvas, we must define to whom it is addressed, segmenting each value proposition by target or customer, for example, to the company where you work, to your boss, to your customers, etc. – from now on, we will call them customers. We must try to make it as specific as possible, including the context and segmenting it by age, profession, etc. For example, a restaurant's value proposition is not the same for in-store service as it is for home delivery. When you define the segment well, you are more certain that you are developing a value proposition that fits your customer.

Once you have defined your customer, you must appreciate in them:

The customer's jobs: these are the problems they are trying to solve with their activities, the requirements or the activities they intend to finish. Continuing with the same example of the restaurant, if you are thinking about the customer who goes to lunch, what they are looking for is: to share a moment with family, to have a moment of distraction, not to cook at home, to have a nice time, etc.

It is important to mention that you can classify them into four types:

Functional: for example, eating in a restaurant.

Social: in pursuit of status or power. E.g., Feeling proud to be able to eat out with your family.

Personal/emotional: seeking to feel something specific. E.g., Feeling happy and at ease with your family.

Supportive: either as acquisition or consumption of value. E.g., Waiting for a table.

The joys: are the benefits they hope to receive, they can be necessary, expected, desirable or unexpected. E.g., Entertainment for the little ones while waiting for the food, friendliness of the waiter, hot food, good prices, etc.

Frustrations: are those that cause discomfort. E.g., cold food, slow service, loud music, tables too close together, etc.

In this way, we already have clarity on what our customer is looking for, now we must order them according to the degree of importance and then see how we create joy and how we alleviate frustrations by defining with which service or product we solve it. This is how we match what our customer wants and our value proposition.

Complete the diagram below to start building your value proposition.

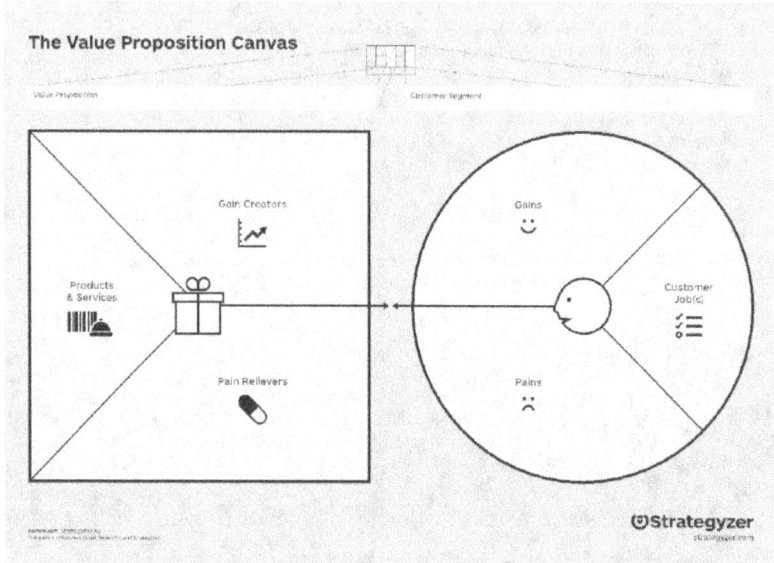

Once we define the value proposition for you to clearly indicate how we are going to generate value, fill in the following:

OUR (products or services)	
HELP(N) (segment)	
WHAT THEY WANT (work)	
FOR	
AND GET	
UNLIKE (competition)	

Identifying the elements that make us different helps us to elaborate a personal strategy that will provide us with security and confidence in our abilities, increasing our adaptive capacity to the constant changes and challenges that come our way, achieving a high level of personal empowerment where we acquire autonomy in decision making and the path we wish to follow.

It is recommended to revisit the form from time to time to ensure you meet the real needs of the end customer or target. As is well known, society and the world are in constant evolution, and so are we, hence the importance of understanding that we cannot remain static.

"Having differentiation does not ensure success, but it does increase our chances of achieving it."

Here are some questions to review the most important aspects of this chapter.

Mobilizing Questions

What are your qualities that people really notice?
_____
_____
_____
_____

Why should they choose you?
_____
_____
_____
_____

What makes you unique?
_____
_____
_____

What value do you bring to your environment?
_____
_____
_____

How do you generate value in what you do?
_____
_____
_____

Do you know the needs of your environment?
_____
_____
_____

What benefits can they achieve with you?
_____
_____
_____

How will I stay current and up-to-date?
_____
_____
_____

Chapter 5
Competitiveness

"Don't Worry, Get Busy."

We all know the word "competitive" and how important it is to remain competitive and positioned at a level that will lead us to meet our objectives faster, deliver value to our profession and in whatever we are doing. It is fundamental to persist in this "race" to always have a competitor as a reference point. I remember when I was a little girl and I ran the four hundred meters - don't get your hopes up, it was only a few interschool competitions, nothing exciting. The first thing I learned is that you should never look back because that's how you lose your advantage. With this I want to take you to think of a triathlon where each competitor has an adversary, who has practically the same skills and has even dedicated the same amount of preparation time, both with the aim of winning the race. Only one can win. Once the race is over, the one who came in second will immediately start to evaluate why they didn't win, what advantage the other had: better preparation, better nutrition, a better coach, a better body structure. Both athletes will have prepared themselves for the race so what was the difference? Maybe the winner never looked back? Maybe the trainer was very good?

From this example, we deduce three elements that are the basis for making our personal brand competent.

1. A sense of competence – competitiveness.
2. Focus on ourselves – self-knowledge.
3. Preparation and learning.

When I talk about having a sense of competence, it is to be convinced that we have what it takes to compete with others. It is to trust and believe in ourselves. We achieve this when we realize that we are capable of solving complex situations, when we obtain the desired results, when we see that we use our resources optimally and when we know where our purpose lies.

Thus, the second idea of focusing on ourselves takes on great importance. It is learning to compete, but against ourselves, constantly reviewing our strengths, enhancing the value we deliver and what our differences are. We must look for ways to improve ourselves day by day, boosting our personal and professional growth, focused on continuous improvement. Sometimes we waste a lot of energy and time observing what people do. Thinking about this point, I am reminded of the Hanna and Barbera cartoons called *Wacky Races*, where there was a character named Dick Dastardly who was more concerned with ensuring his competitors lost than about winning the race. Likewise, he wasted time focusing on the others' weaknesses and not his own, so he always lost. With this I want us to reflect on where we focus and where we place our energies.

It is important to understand that it is not only about being in the race, but also about having consistency to last in the competition. For this, it is necessary to enhance our skills, sustaining them with constant preparation, reinforcing and/or acquiring others, according to the challenges we face. This is a commitment that we have to make to ourselves.

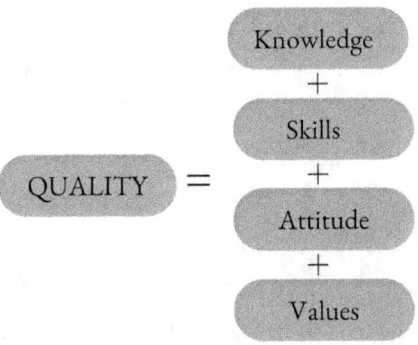

Responsibility

"Don't make excuses; take responsibility."

One element that makes us more competent is how responsible we are with ourselves. Here we should review the concept that it is the "capacity existing in every active subject of law to recognize and accept the consequences of a deed done freely" (RAE). From this quote we can understand that personal responsibility is vital, that our ability to achieve and take charge of our own decisions depends on personal responsibility. We must be clear where we must make our own decisions and take personal responsibility and where starts the responsibility of others. When we understand the limits, we will have clarity and become more effective in the tasks we must perform.

Often, we make ourselves in the victim, justifying what we do not do by blaming others, for example: "I lacked time", "you should also worry about paying the bills", "I asked you to remember me", and I could go on.

We must move away from guilt and victim mentality and

move towards discipline, building our life with a positive attitude towards the capabilities we have and what we must develop to be better. If you have to answer an *e-mail* and you tell your co-worker to remind you to send the *e-mail* and she forgets to do it, whose responsibility is it? Not hers, clearly, it is yours, since you are the only one who knows how important it was.

As we visualize the areas in which we are responsible, we acquire more autonomy and awareness of what corresponds to us and what to the other, setting limits and assuming where we must place attention to be better every day. This is personal responsibility. For this reason, when we fail, we are failing ourselves. This is true in all areas of our lives.

"Whoever wants to do something finds a means, whoever wants to do nothing finds an excuse" Arabic proverb.

Commitment

"Do it and do it right!"

To understand what commitment is, I want us to read the following fable:

A pig and a hen were walking together in a field, when the hen stops for a moment and says to the pig,

"Why don't you and I set up a restaurant?"

"Very good idea! What would it be called?"

"Mmm... Eggs with bacon," proposed the hen.

The pig thought for a while and answered him,

"On second thoughts, better not, it's preferable that you and I don't go into business."

"Why not? I really liked the idea," says the hen, "What made you change your mind?"

"It's simple; if you and I opened a restaurant, I would be totally committed, but you would only be involved."

Moral: the pig was right; it is not the same to put a few eggs than all the meat on the grill. When you commit, you give it all.

Commitment goes beyond getting involved, it is wanting to do it and giving one hundred percent, it is born from us having the certainty that we want to carry it out. When we acquire a personal commitment, we feel more motivated, it assures us better results and learning. When we carry out an activity or perform a role only out of a sense of obligation, it is easier to lose motivation and we quickly become frustrated. We must do things based on commitment.

What if we are doing something we do not like? In this case, let's look for the benefit we derive from it, be it economic, social, third party and/or personal, accepting it as a way to what we aspire to. This helps to maintain a good attitude, which leads us to take control of our time and our life, enhancing autonomy.

When we commit ourselves, we transform our promises into reality, expressing that confidence to our environment and into what we do, thus becoming leaders and leveraging our competencies.

Learning

We reviewed in the previous chapter the importance of learning when it comes to differentiating ourselves, and it will also have an impact on our domains.

To understand the true value of learning, it is important to distinguish between knowledge and learning. The former is about knowing about something, it implies only having information about something. There are people who know a great deal, who inform themselves through different means such as reading, the internet, lectures, etc., but do not apply their knowledge to life; this is where learning makes a big difference.

Learning is centered on that experience acquired through constant practice; to achieve significant learning, we must unite it with the emotional. When we see changes in us, that information has been integrated.

If we remain dedicated to learning, even in complex situations, taking from them an opportunity to grow, we will boost our talents. We should never be complacent with our level of learning, but keep working, making a personal commitment to learn, investing time in our personal and professional growth.

Good Habits

Creating good habits means creating routines so that they become part of us. The brain, in its eagerness to simplify, find new stimuli or simply relax, loves to turn routines into habits. It sounds beneficial for us, but we have to be careful with those rest periods that our brain takes so that it does not overlook something important.

Among the differences between a person who manages to compete and one who does not, is the creation of habits that favor the activity or role he/she performs. That is why it is important for all areas of our lives to form routines that leverage our development and performance. They can be ignored, changed or replaced, but be careful, they cannot be eliminated.

There is a golden rule for changing habits described by Charles Duhigg in his book *The Power of Habits*, who proposes that there are three components to habits:

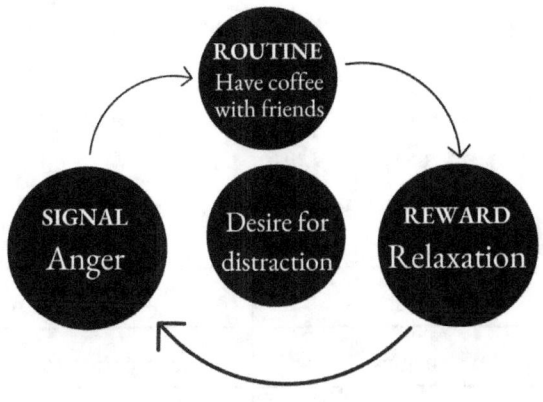

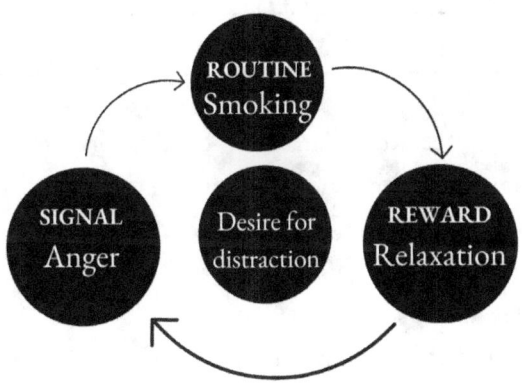

Signal: It is the one that initiates the behavior.

Routine: the behavior itself or habit.

Reward: what makes you want to do that behavior again.

To change a routine, identify the signal or what makes you act that way, describe the reward, and then, work to modify the habit without changing the reward. If a person, every time he is bored at work, checks social networks because he gets the reward of connecting with his friends and being entertained, he can change it only if he finds another element that entertains him, such as, for example, a *coffee break* with a colleague friend.

I recommend practicing this model to change those habits that do not bring personal benefit. Here is a list to start integrating in your life and achieve a better personal wellbeing, which will influence your competences.

Gratitude	Resting time
Plan your tasks	Allocate time for reflection
Organize your workplace	Collaborate in an activity
Observe your environment	Make a gesture of generosity
Speak to yourself with affection	Greetings looking into the eyes

As we can see, there are four dimensions: responsibility, commitment, learning and good habits that we focus on to enhance our faculties. These give us coherence between what we are and what we do, highlighting the elements that allow us to compete with professionals in our field. Our confidence is boosted by having more resources to take on new challenges, achieving well-being with us and strongly leveraging our competencies.

How Can We Identify Our Competencies?

To define them, we must look at which of our capabilities comprises these four elements:

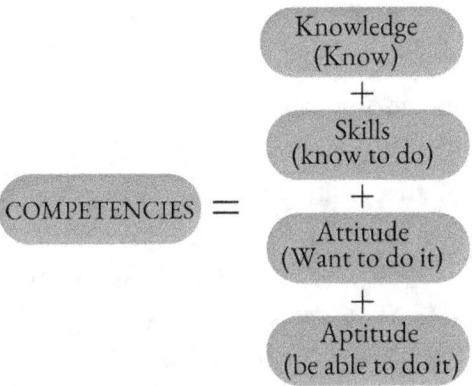

Self-awareness	
Awareness of others	
Self-management	
Inspirational leadership	
Critical thinking	
Emotional intelligence	
Cognitive flexibility	
Creativity	
Troubleshooting	
Serving orientation	

Discovering our competencies makes us recognize that we have, depending on the context, an advantage over our peers. Broadening the vision we have of our competencies enables us to build a personal strategy that gives us great adaptability to the challenges we face, developing the ability to offer a quality version for that role or activity and meeting the expectations of us.

Our faculties can be fostered at different levels, being specific to our objectives. That is why it is essential to observe which are necessary in the area of our interest in order to identify, implement and strengthen those that are suitable to position us at an advantage over others.

From this list above, identify those that you observe in yourself by marking them with blue; those that you would like to have, with orange; those that you should have, with red; and those that you admire in others, with green. This exercise should be done separately for each role or activity you perform and remember, there is room for you to add others.

Once marked, start generating routines that will help you drive them.

Here are some questions to help activate what we have reviewed in this chapter and prepare us to move on to the next.

Mobilizing Questions

What is the real challenge in this activity?
_____
_____
_____
_____

What competencies do I need to develop?
_____
_____
_____
_____

What habits are holding me back?
___
___
___
___

In what areas of life do I feel satisfied?
___
___
___
___

What have I stopped doing for a long time, why?
___
___
___
___

How am I organizing my time?
___
___
___
___

Do I feel competitive?
___
___
___
___

Chapter 6
The Key to Success

As we have seen in the previous chapters, in all the roles we play, not only technical knowledge is required, but also certain personal and social skills that facilitate our activities and, in turn, benefit interpersonal relationships. A lack of these skills leads to poor management of our emotions and behaviors, resulting in decisions that may not be entirely optimal for us. In this chapter, we will review one of the most important competencies to relate to others and adequately convey what we want: communication.

To understand how relevant communication is, it is important to recognize that we are currently immersed in a world where digitalization has become almost essential in many, if not all, areas of our lives. Have you ever had an argument via text message? Have you had a misunderstanding with your partner or your circle of friends through some messaging app? Now, would you rather text than talk on the phone? I imagine most of the answers will be yes. Few are spared from this profound virtual age and its impact on interpersonal relationships. However, we must not lose sight of the fact that behind the technology are the people who use technological elements for more direct communication with the whole world, a means by which we are forming links and networks.

These links are marked by the quality of our communication to the point of opening and/or closing doors. It is interesting to see that very few of us recognize that this is where the main obstacle to our personal development and growth lies. Nobody taught us the value of knowing how to express to others what we are and what we do, assuming that the correct way is the one we see in our closest environment. We do this instinctively without truly understanding its importance.

It is clear that such skills and knowledge allow us to advance in our work and personal lives, therefore we can assume that integrating new personal and social skills is also important if we hope to be accepted in our environment, form better bonds and facilitate interaction in such a way that generates a positive effect on the differentiation of our personal brand and well-being. These skills are constantly evolving and are mainly influenced by context, experiences and learning, adapting and improving based on each area of our life. This is where we sometimes fail to understand why people perceive us in an unfavorable light.

Regardless of whether we are competent or not, if we do not communicate correctly, we can send the wrong messages of who we are and what we do, losing or contaminating our personal and work relationships.

What happens then when we say one thing and people seem to hear something else? This is where misinterpretation, frustration and certain conflicts arise. What does the receiver understand? What does the sender understand? What does the environment perceive? What do I understand to have happened?

Communication is a process that is part of the history and culture of each country, constituting its identity and influencing us in the same way. This bidirectional procedure makes it possible to exchange information between sender and receiver through various common elements, where both verbal and nonverbal messages are issued, and both get constant feedback.

Every communicative act has a purpose in which basic elements interact: sender, receiver, code, channel and message.

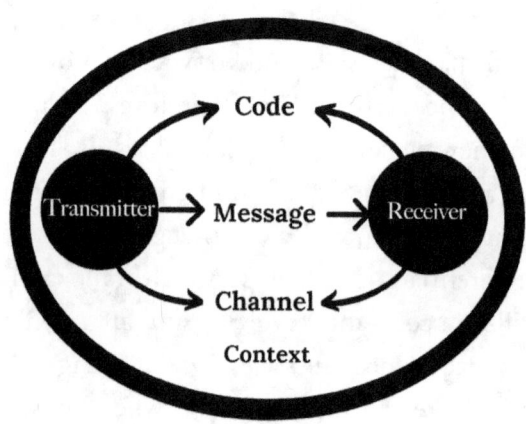

Based on this, we develop different types of communication: journalistic communication, assertive, aggressive, digital, political, emotional, among many others. Regardless of the type of communication, it is a priority to communicate effectively in order to have an impact on the receiver and our environment.

Communication skills are important at all stages of our lives, as they are directly linked to how we form relationships and bonds.

Thus, perfecting our communication consciously serves us in any context of our lives. Yes, this will probably sound crazy and far-fetched, but if we consider what may be the most transcendental elements of the human being, we will realize that it is language. In its different ways of expression and diverse languages, it has promoted a need to communicate with each other, even if we do not speak the same language, we seek to make our ideas known to another.

Effective communication seeks to transmit messages in a clear and convincing way, in order to fulfill the objectives expected by the sender to the receiver and vice versa. Its main benefit is to avoid misinterpretations and misunderstandings of the message, which can lead to problems or failures in our interpersonal relationships. The main purpose is to combine all the elements involved in the message so that they cohere in order to create a better understanding.

Now, is learning to communicate effectively the key to success? That's right, we are in an integrated world where every day it is more important to develop communication in order to achieve a more fluid channel of understanding. The good management of communication networks and a strategic structure of them will allow you to move in the direction you want, aligning with your surroundings.

We must understand that communication is not a master key that opens all doors, and with that I want us to understand that we must make a key for each individual door, modifying and adapting it according to what we want to open.

Effective communication can be learned, generating habits so that it is projected in a natural way. To do this, we have to focus on different skills that, as a whole, make the communication process much more understandable so that when connecting with the personal or work environment, it enables the creation of communication bridges that originate links so that we are recognized and remembered. This enhances our security, resulting in better performance, competitiveness and differentiation that impact our personal brand.

Expressing our emotions is to deliver to the another, through our way of being, our knowledge and skills, in a flexible way in order to build valuable process of communication.

A closer look at the full act of communication, is important to implement an effective strategy.

Primary Elements in Communication

Receiver

When elaborating our message, we must keep our receiver or audience in mind. Design and structure the message so that it can be received and interpreted correctly. Here it is of great importance that we have references and knowledge. It is important to avoid misinterpretations and, even, misunderstandings that harm the communicative process. Some references to consider are:

Expectations: we must unite what the receiver expects and the objective of the message in order to meet our own expectations, as well as those of our receiver. This is how we will design a message that contains the elements they expect to receive. I do not know if it has happened to you, but sometimes we sign up for a talk or workshop where the title does not match the reality. There can be strong disappointment or discouragement, confidence in the speaker is broken. In reference to this issue, the important thing is to be clear what our message is going to contain so that we do not lose that valuable link.

Language: know the language, idioms and technical terms so that the message delivered to your receiver is understandable.

Channel: choose the most friendly and trustworthy communication channel so that the receiver is willing to receive your message. We have different channels to communicate: written message, image, social networks, telephone, event, etc.

Context: check what is the most appropriate environment, whether it is a group of people or an individual. We all feel more comfortable in certain spaces and places. Informing us of this gives a sign of empathy to our receiver. If we have the possibility to ask, it is better to do so. Thus, when elaborating our message, we will not only consider the precision of the target, but also the timing of the message, adjusting it to the specific context and audience.

Message

We must be clear about what we want to transmit and the result we want to obtain. Communication is about expressing thoughts and ideas with the intention of producing change in a situation or simply to deliver a message correctly.

It is not enough to have knowledge and/or experience to achieve the results we are looking for with that message, we must also consider the following factors:

Language: (verbal language and its resources are detailed below) both parties must recognize and understand the language used. The message must be constructed with inclusive language and be rich in content. If we are going to speak in front of an audience, we must consider whether it is necessary to translate the message.

Assertive content: express the message a direct way, ensuring that it arrives with precision, integrating in it what we want to deliver and the added value we provide. Our message must be expressed with strength and conviction to be powerful. We must be aware that words have power and be determined to share them with others. Assertive messages are built respecting one's own rights as well as those of the audience, articulating ideas and emotions honestly, without forgetting the needs of the other, without judging or disqualifying anyone, always calm and confident. We must be able to contribute constructively when conflicts arise.

Structure: the message is designed in such a way that the receiver remains attentive and interested, for this reason, it is important to plan it and give it a structure to fulfill our objectives. A message to sell does not have the same structure as a message to explain a new process.

Clarity and simplicity: our message must have a clear and simple vocabulary for the listener. By this I mean that the idea we want to convey must be clearly structured, do not assume your message is obvious. We must always consider that the listener may know nothing about the subject so be clear in order to avoid misunderstandings and misinterpretations. This is where we often fail with the people closest to us, leading to ruptures in the most important links. Let's remember that communication is bidirectional, therefore, the other person also has something to share.

Motivation: to sustain motivation we must be able to maintain the receiver's attention. It is essential to have a good attitude towards the communicative process, where our message has to be conveyed energetically, bringing out the best in us – you have to believe the story, keep your mood high and share that energy with – without exaggeration of course. Keep your mind on the environment to be aware when you start to lose your audience (read the nonverbal language).

Verbal language

Verbal language is essential to transmit ideas, thoughts and feelings. It reflects our experience, culture and learning. For everyone, it can be seen as something very simple, but it is a complex procedure influenced by multiple factors that we must keep in mind when we want to communicate effectively, structuring and designing the message in a convincing way, sustaining the precision of the words and assuming a common language or linguistic code. Attention must go a step further, paying attention to the content of substance and form, considering that words have power, the idea is to get to express our message directly and with respect, being responsible for the words we use.

To facilitate the communicative process, consider the following resources:

Paraphrasing: the message is expressed in our own words or simple expressions, adding comments or opinions to expand the message, highlighting the main ideas without changing its meaning, seeking to be understood and interpreted by the receiver.

Example: "Choose a job you like, and you will never have to work a day in your life" Confucius.

Paraphrase: if you like your job, you will do it happily without feeling obligation.

Avoid rambling: straying from the main idea of your message makes your recipient lose interest or become confused. Always keep the focus on the message and what you want to deliver.

Tone of voice: keep a pleasant and natural tone to prevent your receiver becoming bored. This can require training.

Forget prejudices: our anticipated opinion of the receiver, pigeonholed by profession, job or standing in life, can give us an erroneous or negative idea of someone. Prejudice can prevent connection and hinder communication.

Example: "As a lawyer, I imagine you don't have time to have fun."

Feedback: in the process of verbal communication, *feedback* is of special importance. It allows us to understand if our message has been correctly received, if the receiver understands, agrees or disagrees with us. It is necessary to measure the effectiveness of our message and to then fine tune it to reduce future possibility of misinterpretation.

Empathy: to put oneself in, and understand, another person's place, from their emotions to their behavior. Empathy is one of the most recognized and demanded skills in society, possessing it makes it easier for us to connect with others, creating communication bridges enriching our message. This skill, like many others, can be honed. Try adding certain personal details or shared experiences that make the receiver connect with the information we are conveying. Little by little, it will become a habit that becomes part of each of the communicative processes that we carry out. Empathy has a positive impact on the receptivity of our message, facilitating the connection with the receiver by generating their trust towards us.

Nonverbal language

This kind of communication clearly expresses what we feel or think by means of non-linguistic signs, that is, signs that are not mediated by spoken or written language. These are performed unconsciously and at high speed by movements of our body and face. To understand these non-linguistic signs, we have to reinforce our self-awareness of the messages we are delivering in order to better understand and manage our interaction with others. They can give us information about our receiver, so they are very useful when we want to understand how someone is receiving our message and when it is time to calibrate to maintain the connection.

Observe body movements and gestures carefully because they provide accurate information about other people. It is not enough for us to see someone cross their arms to believe that they are not interested in what we are talking about, we must observe also the eyes, body movements, etc. It seems simple, but we must take the whole of what we are interpreting, otherwise, this can lead us to a breakdown in communication.

For the story to be properly perceived, these non-linguistic signs must be consistent with our message. Some factors that influence nonverbal language are:

Kinesthetic: the focus on facial and body movements, posture, types of gaze, gaze holding and body contact, to and from us.

Proxemics: the spatial relationship and interaction distance between the sender and the receiver. Four zones are considered to exist: the intimate zone (fifty centimeters apart); the personal zone (120 centimeters apart); social zone (three meters apart); and public zone (more than three meters apart). This can vary depending on culture.

Chronemic: related to the use of time and how it is organized, the importance given to time or the concept that each person has of it, differentiated mainly by culture. We can find punctual and non-punctual people, with others who divide their time for each activity and some who do several activities without differentiating the time for each one, or also with those who allocate a certain amount of time for some activities: events, greetings, hugs, etc. Let's remember that, nowadays, we have more interaction with different cultures, making it very important to have knowledge of the chronemics of our receiver to structure our message appropriately.

Diacritic: personal image and dress codes. Taking care of our personal image goes beyond how we dress, since it refers, among other things, to our personal care, how we walk, personal style, gestures, tone of voice, behavior, etc. We must seek a balance in our appearance in order to stand out without excess. There must be coherence between the message and the image that is transmitted.

Paralinguistic: these are the non-linguistic vocal elements that accompany the message. They are considered nonverbal because they depend on our state of mind, our emotions or intentions. They include the volume, rhythm, diction and emphasis of the voice.

Active Listening

Knowing how to listen can be considered one of the most important elements in the communicative process. Listening is often overlooked as a communication technique. One of the reasons for not listening carefully is the fear of being influenced by others, believing that we are the owners of the truth and thinking that by speaking we generate more influence than by listening.

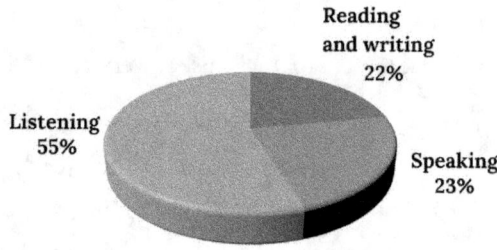

According to researchers, the total time we spend on communication is eighty percent, which is divided into:

Actually, we spend more time listening than talking. In his research on emotional intelligence, Goleman identified the art of listening as one of the main skills of people with high levels of emotional intelligence. He considers it as the first of the skills that determine the management of relationships, which makes it possible to understand others, including perceiving other people's feelings and perspectives and taking an active interest in their concerns. The practice of active listening develops skills that enhance our emotional intelligence.

First of all, we must differentiate between hearing and listening: According to the Royal Spanish Academy (RAE), the first meaning of hearing is "to perceive sounds with the ear", while the definition of listening is "to pay attention to what is heard." What this means, in other words, is that listening is not only a biological function that depends on our auditory acuity, but also implies a voluntary act, where we are paying attention to what is heard. Although it may seem obvious, it is essential to emphasize that it is possible to hear without listening and that, in order to listen, we must also observe.

Listening to another person demonstrates availability, receptivity and understanding of what they say, both in words and in tone of voice and body language. It requires observing with interest, not interrupting and avoiding prejudices. Active listening creates a climate of trust and helps to avoid misunderstandings. Misunderstandings are the cause of most conflicts and are the precursors to all forms of violence. Listening is a process that involves other variables of the subject: attention, interest, motivation, etc. It is an active act that is much more complex than the simple passivity that we associate with not speaking.

What does it depend on to feel welcomed when communicating our emotions?

It is important for us that the receiver feels welcomed in their emotions. If when someone explains their emotions to us, we tend to minimize them, question them, judge them or interrupt their speech to give them advice or ask multiple questions, it is likely that the person will end up inhibiting their emotions and potentially believe that their thoughts and emotions are neither appropriate nor valid.

If we listen with compassion or with excessive emotionality, without helping to adopt different points of view, we will generate in the person a fixation of that emotion and the associated thoughts, preventing them from evolving.

Robertson (1994), a scholar and consultant on these issues, wrote, "We all think listening is important, but how many of us do it well? I would report that it would be rare to find one in a hundred senior executives who was a really good listener. Many people focus their attention on what they are going to say after the other person finishes speaking. They don't even try to check what they think they have heard, let alone recognize tone or emotional nuances. These are fundamental errors in employing this basic skill. Regardless of your education or experience, you must learn to listen..."

Specialists agree that knowing how to listen is one of the most difficult skills to find and acquire because, among other things, it requires "putting oneself in the place of others," putting aside, even temporarily, one's own paradigms and assuming that others may see things differently. When we listen, we must also control our own emotional responses to what we hear, perhaps things that don't fit with our version of reality. This is a skill that requires a willingness to learn and change.

"It takes courage to stand up and speak. But much more to sit and listen" Winston Churchill.

Active listening is a technique derived from therapy, centered on the person that originates from the humanistic psychologist Carl Rogers and others. Rost, in his 2002 book *Teaching and Researching*, defined it as "a generic term to define a series of behaviors and attitudes that prepare the receiver to listen, to concentrate on the person speaking and to provide feedback". It also implies, among other things, making oneself available and showing interest in the person speaking. Active listening consists of communication that demonstrates to the speaker that the listener has understood him/her. It refers to the ability to listen to what the person is expressing directly and to pay attention to the feelings, ideas or thoughts that underlie his or her expression.

Active listening involves understanding the subjective

experience of the speaker and being able to effectively communicate that understanding. We must avoid distractions and focus on listening without letting them influence our thoughts.

Another author to consider is Edgar Schein (1995), a reference in organizational communication, who states that "interrupting others is one of the most common and destructive communication behaviors. Most people have little awareness of how frequently and rudely they interrupt others, convinced that they have something more important to say than what the speaker is about to say."

Active listening techniques

The ability to really listen is more difficult to find and to perfect than that of being a good communicator. According to specialists being able to listen well aids communication, provides more authority and influence and therefore helps us to achieve our objectives. This skill helps us not only to understand what the person wants to express, but also to understand the feelings, ideas or thoughts that underlie what they are saying. Active listening means listening and understanding communication from the point of view of the speaker.

The most common mistake made is to want to speak first and express our point of view at all costs, so that we concentrate only on the idea we want to convey, and not on what we are being told. This form of distraction is seriously detrimental to communication.

We have to work on the skills required to achieve active listening:

Silence: this is the most difficult skill, since we generally want to share our point of view and experiences to demonstrate that we have the knowledge of what the other is talking about and that we can effectively lead them to their goals. We must remain silent, avoiding intervening in the story by expressing feelings and asking questions.

Silence should be welcoming, positive, warm and offer signs that you are actively accompanying their progress.

Practice will lead us to know when it is time to be silent and listen before speaking. Silence is part of our emotional intelligence.

Respecting space: not interrupting others when they are talking is part of maintaining the space for reflection. This process depends on each one of us. It means letting them speak without anticipating what they are going to say. Our intervention should come after requesting permission from the other person. Intervening in this silence should be brief and strategic. Also, do not place value or judge the other's words immediately. Asking permission also makes the *other* pay full attention to the interruption.

Some questions you can use when you want to intervene are:
May I interrupt you?
Can I ask you a question?
I would like to comment on something, may I?

Could I ask you a question on this matter?

Attention to the story: in order for our receiver to feel that we are interested or attentive to their opinion, we must take into account our nonverbal communication, such as our posture, head nodding, gaze, distractions, etc.

To acquire this skill, it is important to consider the following:
Avoid distractions - looking at the time, cell phone, etc.
Try to repeat some words or phrases that have just been said.
Rephrase some of the statements in the story.

Ask for clarification if you do not understand.
Empathize.
Do not judge.
Express in our own words what you have understood from the message.
Some proposed questions:
So, as I see it, what was going on was that...?
You mean you felt...?

When such a thing happened..., were you...?

Feedback: the ability to give and receive feedback increases the possibilities for a rich communicative process.

By paying attention to the topics that the other person is interested in, always avoiding talking about oneself, we can internalize this competence. We must reinforce positive behaviors and motivate others.
Some questions you can use at this point are:
What of all this is useful for you to...?
How would you use this in...?

Feedback should include inquiry that makes it possible to hear and understand the receiver's point of view. It is necessary to compare the interpretation of the facts with the message we wish to convey.

Empathy: we must avoid a hostile and emotional attitude. Empathy provides us with the expression of understanding of ideas and feelings, this will help the receiver to feel heard, stimulating him to speak and express himself in an easy way (Manning, Reece, 1997).

In the book "*The 7 Habits of Highly Effective People*", Covey lays out the principles of empathetic communication, noting that when another person speaks, we usually listen at one of four levels:

1. Ignore, do not listen to it at all.
2. Pretense. "Yeah, right, right."
3. Selective listening, hearing only certain parts of the conversation.
4. Attentive listening, paying attention and focusing all our energy on the words being spoken.

For this author, empathic listening must enter into the other person's frame of reference, see things through that world, as the other person appreciates them, understand their paradigm, identify what they feel. Covey clarifies that "empathy is not sympathy," specifying that sympathy is a form of agreement or judgment, which is sometimes the most appropriate emotion and response. But "people often thrive on sympathy, which makes them dependent."

The essence of empathic listening is not about agreeing, but about deeply and completely understanding the other person, both emotionally and intellectually, and includes much more than registering, reflecting and even understanding the words spoken. "In empathic listening," says Covey, "you listen with your ears, but also [and this is more important] with your eyes and with your heart. You listen to the feelings, to the meanings."

Resources for active listening

We will take some resources proposed by Ariel Goldvarg in an article entitled, "What you understood was not what I said":

Verify: language is ambiguous and can lead to confusion. Verifying what the other person heard allows us to recognize the degree of understanding of what we said and vice versa. Failure to check what was said leads to many misunderstandings.

Avoid assumptions: what is obvious to us may not be obvious to the other person. Standards change with people. Assuming that the other person will interpret exactly what we say can be dangerous. Avoiding assumptions means being alert to what we consider obvious.

Tune in to the other: many times, we assume that people think and interpret things as we do. This causes frustration and separates us. We may not say it in words, but our thoughts and attitudes give us away. If we look at our navel when we speak, it is likely that the other person will do the same. That is why it is important to connect with our interlocutor.

Advantages that active listening has both on the person who listens and on the person who feels listened to:

- It creates a climate of trust and closeness that facilitates mutual understanding.
- Acceptance can be communicated, and motivation can be increased.
- Tension and differences are reduced.
- You learn from each other.
- Conflict reduction is facilitated.
- Helps to make better decisions with greater security.
- You learn to work better.
- You gain time to think.
- User cooperation is encouraged.

Secondary Elements in Communication

These depend on the context and circumstances in which the communicative process takes place, some of which are:

- Physical space
- Ambient noise
- Ambient music
- Temperature/climate
- State of mind of sender and receiver
- Thoughts
- Prejudice

By paying attention to the primary and secondary elements, we are more likely to gain understanding and receive *feedback* more effectively. These elements should be considered important factors in communication. By focusing on each of them consciously and integrating them, we are moving towards a dialogue that allows the message to be understood and grasped by the person receiving it. That our communication contains elements that activate the five senses ensures success in the whole procedure.

Each of the elements we have seen leads us to communicate effectively, so that we can fulfill our objectives and purposes, thus achieving the expected results. The more attention we pay to our communication, the more differentiating elements we will find in ourselves. Indeed, as we well appreciate, there are times when not everything depends on how we prepare ourselves, we must also be able to observe the other empathetically.

Each and every one of the actions described here adds or subtracts in communication, putting our reputation and leadership at stake. Therefore, it is important to pay attention because how you communicate leaves an indelible mark in the memory of the people with whom you interact. Projecting security and confidence makes our personal brand differentiated, credible and successful.

These questions will then be useful in reviewing the highlights of this chapter.

Mobilizing Questions

What elements do you consider when designing and structuring your message?
___
___

Do you know the individual to whom your message is addressed?
___
___
___

What context is most conducive to you?
___
___
___

Are you aware of the way you communicate?
___
___

Do you understand the power of communication?
___
___
___

What elements are you missing?
___
___

Have you considered working on your communication?

_____
_____
_____
_____

Which of the elements described in this chapter do you wish to improve?

_____
_____
_____
_____

What step do you commit to take today?

_____
_____
_____
_____

If you think of a time when you felt your message was successful, what elements did it contain?

_____
_____
_____
_____

Chapter 7
Living Your Personal Brand

Have you noticed that we live in an era of communication, but sometimes it feels like it has become the communications revolution where communication skills will significantly impact the success of any individual's personal and professional relationships. By this I mean that it is essential to build communication strategies to transmit a solid image of our personal brand to the environment around you. It is imperative that you are aware and can deliver all of yourself to generate the effect you are looking for.

By incorporating such strategies, you will be the leader in many aspects, because you will gain trust and credibility. This expansion matters not only in traditional spaces, but in the digital realm, where we have new platforms and decentralized types of communication where *offline* and *online* come together, which requires us to remain constantly alert to new methods of, and tools for, communication.

In this communication strategy, we must not forget the importance of the perception of all those who participate in this communicative process. Likewise, we must always bear in mind that an idea of our message will be built and that this will influence the projection of our personal image. This perception involves all the senses of our audience, so it is vital to put into action all the elements mentioned in the previous chapter to reap the results we want and leave a mark on others.

Aristotle, more than 2300 years ago, spoke of three parts of communication: *ethos*, *pathos* and *logos*. He defined them as the pursuit of "all the means of persuasion at our disposal," making it very clear that the main goal of the communicative process is to persuade, that is, to bring others to share the same point of view as the speaker.

Personally, and in my experience, not all of us are looking for that, rather, we want to understand and to be understood, not necessarily convincing others of our point of view, since many of us also seek to inform, entertain, make people aware, etc. At this point, it is very important to understand that creating and delivering a good communication has to do with being efficient and effective in delivery, since we can find a variety of communicative models according to the different intentions.

This is how we will focus on some elements that will give us the tools for effective communication, expressing what we think coherently and fluently. The idea is to help our receiver, as the word says, to remain receptive. It is about keeping them motivated with our message by adding skills, emotions and attitude.

Personal and Professional Image

The personal and professional image is what our personal brand denotes visually, how our listener perceives us through their eyes. It is important to remember that, according to studies, fifty-five percent of your image is determined by your appearance; thirty-eight percent by your nonverbal communication; and seven percent by what is said about you. So, keep in mind that ninety-three percent of this impression is determined by what we project.

The first impression is produced in only four seconds, that is the time we have to form a mental image of you. After that we have approximately twenty-six seconds to make our receiver change that first perception.

It is very difficult to change that first impression because the brain maintains the perception it received in those first seconds, trying to confirm it by searching for evidence, and ignoring that which contradicts. The way we are perceived, and the accuracy of this first impression is a very powerful idea that will determine the bonds we form with people.

Most of our image is generated by what people see, that is why we must work on it, properly selecting our logo, colors, personal appearance, clothing, social networks presentation, etc., everything that enters through the eyes. For this reason, it is important to spark the receiver's interest in what we are saying and to help them to visualize a coherence of what we say.

It is a point to pay great attention to. In this *personal branding* program, we take care of the personal and professional image to achieve that first impression of impact, focusing on your image and communication, gaining that ninety-three percent.

Verbal and Nonverbal Communication in Action

Or "How your body expresses itself when we are communicating our message." One of the instances where we put into practice everything we know about verbal and nonverbal communication is when we have to speak in front of people. Usually, we believe that just because we know the subject we have to talk about, we are prepared. This is the first mistake, since the last thing we should do is to boast about everything we know. Rather, we have to connect with our audience and create a bond that generates trust and confidence.

In 2018, *Forbes* mentions in an article the importance of our speech creating that link with brief and powerful content, called KISS (*keep it short and simple*). On many occasions, we are clear about what we want to say, but what happens when we have to prepare a speech? In this situation, we are looking for the listeners to maintain their motivation and interest and to empathize with our message, that is, to identify, understand or agree with our ideas. Another reason to throw a "kiss" to the audience is the case of social networks as a means of dissemination. You should seek to deliver that fragment effectively, adjusted to the platform used, whether Instagram, Facebook, YouTube, Pinterest, and even through email.

When you prepare your speech, it is important to place yourself in the now and highlight the reason why you are delivering that message at that particular moment. The first question you should answer in your speech is: what is the importance of being here today? Then, as you develop it, the speech needs two clear points: the what and the how you say it.

The idea is to tell a good story that contains added value within the message you are delivering.

The structure of your speech should contain:

Introduction: right from the start, the speech must capture the interest and attention of the audience. This is where you guide the listener to the content of the speech. You can start with an anecdote, ask questions, use a strong phrase, a quote that highlights your message. We must be able to influence with our image, nonverbal communication and then with our words.

Metaphors: it is a resource that you apply in your speech by transferring what you think and that you build with words, determining the meaning it will have. The metaphor shapes people's thinking, so that, depending on the connotation of our speech, we will use it with the aim of predisposing your audience to take the attitude that benefits the dissemination of your message.

"Flocks of seabirds coming from the south, rosaries of dawn in distant silence". Rómulo Gallegos, *Canaima*.

Quotations: these create more confidence in your message by attributing the idea to another author providing more weight to the speech. Do not exaggerate and use references of this sort only when necessary or relevant.

Repetition or resonance: the main difference between this and paraphrasing is that repetition is the reiteration of the same thing literally or with a formal variation, in order to recapture an important part of the speech that has been previously said, so that the receiver or audience can grasp the true meaning of the speech.

Enumeration: allows us to order ideas, generating a sequence in our speech, making it more understandable to the receiver. We can use connectors such as: "first of all", "lastly".

Question strategies: questions make connection with the receiver or your audience, these can be open or closed depending on the intention of our message.

Musicality: rhythm and progression. Communicate it uniquely and with passion. The tone of voice is very important to make an impact on the other person. Speak slowly and clearly to attract the listener's confidence. Emphasize certain words to give more effect to the speech and capture the audience's attention; pronounce words correctly, emphasizing the right syllables and consonants; move your lips slowly, a stiff jaw chokes the voice, and an immobile tongue strangles it. Correctly varying the tone and rhythm keeps the speech from being monotonous and boring. Beware of crutches such as "eeeh", "aah", "unh", "umm", etc., the only thing they do is dirty your speech and detract from your professionalism.

- *Punctuation*: respect punctuation. The timing of punctuation in our speech gives meaning to what we say. When we prepare our speech, we must consider the punctuation so that the message is conveyed clearly.
- *Emotional progression:* to help our audience progress towards the emotional state our message requires.
- *Breathing*: Breathing through the diaphragm is important to project a confident voice. It is recommended that before starting to speak we sigh deeply to feel calmer.
- *Silences*: allow the listener to reflect on the content delivered in the message.

When we think of people who have left their mark on us and on the world, such as Martin Luther King, Winston Churchill, Nelson Mandela and Mahatma Gandhi, among others, we come to the conclusion that they have sought that connection with the receiver and all these elements described as great communicators.

During the communicative process, make gestures that open communication such as showing the palms of your hands. Avoid crossing your arms or legs, as this is considered to be a posture of rejection or a closed mind. Maintain eye contact with each of the people participating. Use an appropriate tone of voice that demonstrates your security and confidence. The smile is a great tool, it indicates empathy and openness.

Before presenting a speech, it is important to organize the ideas we want to present, rehearse in front of a mirror and thus observe ourselves and correct elements that we consider necessary. It is also necessary to practice breathing and pausing, as well as to choose a means of communication that is comfortable both for us and for the listener or audience.

Each of these elements mentioned above will make us feel more confident and at ease when presenting a speech.

Presentations

Include powerful *storytelling*, make it personal, generate emotions, arouse curiosity. Use the 10-20-30 rule for your presentations: maximum ten slides, twenty minutes long and use a font size of thirty points or more.

Use powerful body language with an upright posture, shoulders back and your face at a ninety-degree angle facing forward. Make eye contact with your audience and make your arm movements from the waist up.

Fear of Public Speaking

Let's study which skills help us to produce a communicative process rich in elements that make those to whom you are speaking feel comfortable.

Elaboration of the Elevator Pitch

The concept was coined by Philip B. Crosby in the eighties. The author used this as a way to describe condensing an attention-grabbing message into a few seconds or minutes, i.e., the length of an elevator ride, resulting in a future interview or meeting with that person, interest in us or our company.

Objective:

Describe your professional or product profile in about one minute
Capture attention
Be convincing
Reflect your personal brand

Must be:

Clear
Concrete
Simple
Singular
Attractive

Contains:

Who you are
Your experience
Skills

Once you are clear on these points, you begin to design your *elevator pitch*, which should start with a surprising statement or attention-getting question: who are you and why are you here, what problems or needs do you address, what do you solve or bring, what main benefit do people take away from interacting with you, why you are the right person or your project is the right one, and finally, a call to action.

It is important that you consider the following:

- To make it coherent and natural-sounding.
- Write it down and read it aloud several times.
- Make the appropriate changes. Some expressions may not

sound right when spoken aloud.
- Do not recite it woodenly.
- It is important to have clear ideas and order.
- Rehearse several times.
- To make different *elevator pitches* for each context.
- It is a brief, simple, forceful and convincing speech.
- Your smile is a great tool, it shows empathy and openness.

Whenever we carry out a communicative process in which we have a personal and professional objective, we must be prepared to use our own tools and augment those necessary for an effective intervention. Remember that information is power. Communicating effectively is the key to success.

Now you have all the ingredients to convey to people what you want them to see in you. This way, you are ready to manage your personal brand.

The following questions will serve as practice on what happened in this chapter:

Mobilizing Questions

Do you know your beliefs and values?
_____
_____
_____

Do you know what you want to give to other people?
_____
_____
_____

Do you recognize the power of your personal brand?

_____
_____
_____
_____

Are you consistent with who you are and your personal brand image?

_____
_____
_____
_____

Are you integrating your competencies?

_____
_____
_____
_____

Are you aware of the impact you have on your environment?

_____
_____
_____
_____

Are you ready for the next level?

_____
_____
_____
_____

Principles of Personal Branding

At the end of the description of this *personal branding* model, I would like to make available the principles that support it. These will be the basis for the application of the model.

- Uniqueness: we are all unique beings, therein lies the value.
- Internal communication: promote personal reflection at each stage.
- Authenticity: in the authenticity of our values lies the coherence of personal brand management.
- Commitment: by applying the model, we generate a personal commitment that will be the basis for advancing in each of the phases.
- Self-awareness: promoting self-awareness during the process will deliver better results.
- Empathy
- Respect
- Responsibility

The application of the model requires preparation and related skills to obtain optimal results. it independently is the first step in managing your personal brand.

Bibliography

Castelló, A. & Castelló, A. (2013). *Communication skills: active listening.* Observatorio Comunicación en Cambio. http://comunicacionencambio.com/escucha-activa/

Robertson, A. (1994). *Knowing how to listen. A guide to business success.* IRWIN Publishing.

Miedaner, T. (2002). *Coaching for success.* Barcelona. Ediciones Urano S. A.

Schein, E. (1995). *Business culture and leadership.* McGraw Hill.

Cloke, K. (1989). "Designing systems for conflict resolution". *Information Series No. 004.* Center for the Study of Management Techniques. University of Havana.

Goleman, D. (1999). *Emotional intelligence in business.*

Davis, K. (1985). *Organizational behavior.* McGraw Hill.

Covey, S. (1998). *The 7 habits of highly effective people.* Editorial Paidós.

-http://www.asociacionaccent.com/informa/09_Tecnicas_HABILIDADES_SOCIALES/EHS04_test_escucha_activa.pdf

Expansion (2018, September 17). "Boost your salary with personal branding." https://expansion.mx/carrera/2018/09/17/aumenta-tu-salario-con-el-branding-personal.

N. (2020, June 15). *Emotional intelligence. Concept, emergence and advantages.* Concept. https://concepto.de/inteligencia-emocional/#ixzz6qvCT6UOH

Cooperrider, D., & Whitney, D. D. (2005). *Appreciative inquiry: A positive revolution in change.* Berrett-Koehler Store.

Consol Vancells (2016). *The brand called you* (in Spanish). 2021, by Consol Vancells. Website: http://consolvancells.net/the-brand-called-you-espanol/

Daniel Goleman (1995). *Emotional Intelligence.* Spanish edition (1996). Editorial Kairós, S. A.

RAE. "Hearing." June 29, 2021. Royal Spanish Academy. Web site: https://dle.rae.es/o%C3%ADr

Sharon Jirikils, I. (2016). *Integrative coaching model.* Ril editores.

Sharon Jirikils, compiler (2020). *Insights from integrative coaching, vol. 2.* Published by Smart Coach International Academy.

Whitmore, J. (2018). *Coaching: the method to improve people's performance.* Ediciones Paidós.

Maxwell, C. John (2003). *How successful people think, change your thinking, change your life.* Grand central pub.

Osterwalder, A. (2015). *Designing the value proposition.* Deusto.

Eichholz, J. C. (2015). *Adaptive capacity: how organizations can survive and thrive in a changing world.* U. Editions.

https://lamenteesmaravillosa.com/el-origen-de-la-frase-conocete-a-ti-mismo-del-templo-de-apolo/

https://es.scribd.com/document/55135794/Conocete-a-Ti-Mismo

Tom Peters (1997). *The brand called you.* Fast Company.

Deivit Wilfredo Reynoso Espinoza (2018). "Factors of executive ethos: identity, identification and differentiation. A theoretical approach. *Journal of research in psychology* (Vol. 21, Issue 1). Universidad Nacional Mayor de San Marcos.

www.ingramcontent.com/pod-product-compliance
Lightning Source LLC
Chambersburg PA
CBHW071210070526
44584CB00019B/2989